A LITTLE LESS THAN ANGELS

Maurice Hogan SSC is a member of the Missionary Society of St Columban. Ordained in 1965, he has served as a missionary in Japan and more recently in Hong Kong and China. He was professor of sacred scripture at St Patrick's College, Maynooth, and a former member of the Pontifical Biblical Commission (1996–2007) as well as director of World Missions Ireland (Pontifical Mission Societies).

A Little Less than
Angels

Sketch of a
Biblical Anthropology

MAURICE HOGAN SSC

VERITAS

Published 2021 by
Veritas Publications
7–8 Lower Abbey Street
Dublin 1
Ireland
www.veritas.ie

ISBN 978 1 84730 990 7

10 9 8 7 6 5 4 3 2 1

A catalogue record for this book is available from the British Library.

Designed by Jeannie Swan, Veritas Publications
Printed in the Republic of Ireland by SPRINT-print Ltd, Dublin

Veritas books are printed on paper made from the wood pulp of
managed forests. For every tree felled, at least one tree is planted,
thereby renewing natural resources.

When I look at your heavens, the work of your fingers, the moon and the stars which you have established: what is man that you are mindful of him, and the son of man that you care for him? Yet you have made him little less than the angels, and you have crowned him with glory and honour. You have given him dominion over the works of your hands; you have put all things under his feet.

Psalm 8:3–6 (LXX)

I praise you, for I am awesomely and wonderfully designed.

Psalm 139:14

TABLE OF CONTENTS

FOREWORD

Anthropology addresses the question that human beings have been asking since the dawn of history: what does it mean to be human? Christian biblical anthropology sees the created order in relation to and revelatory of God. Christian anthropology must be built on the bridge of the Incarnation. Humanity is viewed as orientated towards God. In the words of St Augustine, 'our hearts are restless until they rest in Thee'.

Biblical anthropology investigates the origin, nature and destiny of human beings and of the universe they inhabit. It focuses on the human being, as created by God, in a state of fallenness due to the misuse and abuse of freedom, the state of redemption brought about by Jesus Christ and the hope for the future. Through biblical anthropology, we, as human beings, discover dimensions of our creaturehood, our sinfulness, our experience of redemption and our hope.

Psalm 8 underlines the fact that all creatures reflect the majesty of God. The psalmist asks, 'What is man …?' – a rhetorical question. Man is viewed in relation to God and, because of this, man is the crown of creation. In the Hellenistic world man was viewed as a rational animal, that is, by reference to what is inferior to him, namely the animal kingdom, whereas in Psalm 8 man is defined by what is superior to him, by heavenly beings: 'you have made him little less than the angels'.

Biblical anthropology differs from the secular disciplines and from cultural anthropology. It does not simply consider how people actually live, but also illustrates how people ought to live. Christian anthropology acknowledges that the human person is created in the image and likeness of God (Gn 1:27). It views Jesus of Nazareth as the tangible and authentic *Imago Dei*. Pope John Paul II, quoting *Gaudium et Spes*, states: 'it is only in the mystery of the Word made flesh that the mystery of man truly becomes clear'. When our relationship with God is denied, we have a very impoverished and truncated view of the human being which historically has given rise to human depravity.

> The elimination of God from public life has generated a fear that lurks beneath the surface of modern existence. People have hopes for the future expressed in a secular faith in progress through technology that is regarded as freedom from the constraints of the world and history alike. This goal, however, is illusory and unattainable, for human beings are not God. There will be no healing of our culture if God is not again recognised as the foundation of our entire existence. Only in union with God is human life truly life. (page 184)

Ten years ago, on a visit to Britain, Pope Benedict XVI urged people to maintain respect for religious traditions. This is an enormous challenge in a modern multi-cultural society. Christianity has played a hugely significant role in European civilisation and culture. The speed, however, with which Europe is dismissing and dismantling its Christian heritage must be a cause for deep concern. In the seventeenth century it was rather unusual to imagine the world *without* God. By contrast, in the twenty-first century it is difficult to imagine the world *with* God. In many respects the secularisation of Europe is a result of the failure of religion to dialogue with and challenge the changes which were taking place. Religion offers an explanation of who we are, why we are here, what our purpose is in the world and an interpretation of things that are taking place. Focusing on the changes in the past hundred years alone, we can detect the rapid expansion of human frontiers, such as with the advent of television, computers and the internet as well as developments in mobility. At the same time, however, there are areas where we still feel helpless, for example in the face of volatile and unpredictable financial markets, currency fluctuations and shifting economic climates.

Maurice Hogan is eminently equipped to plumb the depths of biblical anthropology and its significance in contributing to a fuller and richer understanding of the human person as they relate to God, to one another and to the world in our contemporary culture. Doctor Hogan is a former professor of sacred scripture in St Patrick's College, Maynooth, former member of the Pontifical International Biblical Commission and former director of World Missions Ireland. He is the author of the *Biblical Vision of the Human Person: Implications for a Philosophical Anthropology* (Peter Lang, 1994), editor of *Order and History, Volume 1: Israel and Revelation (The Collected Works of Eric Voegelin, Volume 14)* (University of Missouri Press, 2001) and his book *The Four Gospels: Following in the Footsteps of Jesus* (Veritas, 2015) has been widely acclaimed.

While we continue to ask the most fundamental questions of who we are, why we are here and what kind of world we seek to create, we are in the realm of religion. It is a misunderstanding of faith if it is understood only as outlining moral certitudes. Rather, faith is about openness to wonder and awe in our world. God and the human person are not in competition but rather in a relationship of caring fidelity. The God in whom we believe is concerned about the most vulnerable and the most needy in our world. The world in which we live today is riddled with anxiety – an anxiety that has only been intensified in recent times by the shattering experience of the Covid-19 pandemic. The conventional norms of society have been dismantled and it is unable to perform the tasks which it accomplished in the past.

The dominant culture of our lives has been characterised as technological, which would seem to provide us with limitless power and control, yet still we search for something more. We are in a season of transition as we experience the collapse of a world as we have known it. We acknowledge that the value systems by which we have ordered life are now ineffective. Television and technology place the emphasis on the visual, where the image speaks louder than the word.

In the ancient world, the Greeks recognised the inevitability of fate, whereas the Bible recognised and created a theology of hope. The Greeks excelled in a visual culture – art, architecture, theatre – to be captured by the human eye. The Jewish focus, by contrast, was on the non-visual; the God they could not see or capture in images. The book of Deuteronomy placed the emphasis on hearing: 'Hear, Oh Israel: the Lord our God is one Lord' (Deut 6:4). Throughout the book of Deuteronomy, Moses impresses on the people that if they want God to listen to them and hear their cry, they must listen to God. It is interesting to compare and contrast the Hellenistic culture with the Judeo-Christian one. In the Hellenistic culture, tragedy was a powerful literary device; by contrast, in the Jewish world, we were introduced to hope. While religion may be dismissed as a tendency to live with the past, nevertheless, religion properly understood ought to be a form of protest and ensure that we are not held captive either by the past or the present.

As long as religion continues to ask the fundamental questions of who we are, why we are here and what kind of world we wish to hand on to the next generation, it will continue to be relevant to society. We receive significant reminders of this with the loss of civility in our contemporary world. God and the human person do not compete; rather, God empowers us to be his partners in creation. While in the wisdom literature of the Bible Job questions God, he does not lose faith in God. Likewise today, while many may have ceased to believe in God, they nevertheless consider religion a valuable vehicle of expressing a code of values that civilised society requires.

Living in a technological age is a great challenge to entertaining hope. There is always the tendency to absolutise the present, though genuine hope challenges that mentality. A climate of hopelessness among the affluent and the prosperous seems to be increasing. I wonder why? Hope is a very urgent requirement in our modern Western culture. We tend to be preoccupied with order, while this obsession with order frequently silences the voice of hope. The God of the Bible, however, is not enslaved by the present. It is significant that those who promote the status quo are very reluctant to become heralds of hope. In our society today, hopelessness is becoming more prevalent and pervasive. This is an urgent challenge for all of us. Closely related to hope is courage. Meaninglessness and despair are more prevalent and dominant in our society, although frequently this may be hidden behind the facade of bravado.

The God of the Bible creates new social responsibilities which transcend defeat. When the present is regarded as a form of utopia, we can detect a certain hopelessness in mentality. Hope and faith are very closely interrelated. We can become so identified with the present that we lose our sense of identity as members of a faith community who had a past and also have a future beyond the present. I recall a former professor bemoaning the demise of history and the implications of that for the present and the future. The neglect of memory leads to an abandonment of hope. All of this is something our faith must address. The whole history of the people of God is one of a relationship with a caring God who is faithful to his people, who sees them, knows them and intervenes to liberate them from slavery, whether that slavery is political or personal in terms of human sin.

Doctor Hogan will not allow us to forget that society in general, and main-line Church life in particular, is confronted by enormous challenges and must respond for the sake of our common faith and our humanity. Throughout his work, the author acknowledges that while the Christian faith is what best explains human meaning, dignity and destiny, the temptation to disregard this in favour of a materialist, relativist and politically correct world which is ruled by 'the dictatorship of relativism' is enormous. This work is scholarly and cognisant of the nuances of the biblical languages and cultural influences of the ancient Near East. The scholarship translates into providing us with a clear idea of where we have come from, where we are going and how to get there, as it considers the implications of this journey. The wide-ranging competence of the author enables the text to speak for itself so that we are not engaging with the revival of a dead past, but with a living truth which 'will provide an antidote to modern illusions of self-perfection' (page 23).

✠ *Michael Neary*
Archbishop Emeritus of Tuam

PREFACE

We are living at a time of great opportunity. Every day we encounter the genius of human achievements and many impressive signs of progress. Thanks to advances in the medical sciences and in the wide application of technology, we now enjoy a quality of life that was unimaginable even a few generations ago. During the last century, human 'know-how' and dominion over matter have grown in a manner nobody could have predicted. One would have thought that with the abundance of material goods and the ease of communication provided by transport and social media, we would be the happiest people that ever lived on this planet.

Yet, despite these developments, there seems to be a rapid cultural decline that is evident in escalating violence, random shootings, gross materialism and hedonism to dull the pain of a meaningless existence. Today, there is a general feeling of malaise, aimlessness and depression which can be seen in the pervasiveness of suicide in the Western world. The political, cultural and moral crisis has worldwide repercussions due to rapid communication made possible by technology. Europe is busy dismantling its Christian heritage that, as a matter of historical fact, has contributed enormously to what we call European culture.

These brief considerations are sufficient to demonstrate that the problems we face today go to the heart of who and what we are as human beings. It seems that a retrieval of our identity is called for by returning to the sources, among them biblical revelation, that historically have formed the order of individual and social existence in the world. For it is becoming more and more obvious that the future may no longer be one of technological, economic, social and political progress which has been taken for granted until recently. We are reluctantly being awakened from our public unconsciousness of spiritual realities. We are obliged to make room again for the God who created the world to overcome the spiritual void we are living through. A broader vision of life is required to sustain us during our sojourn in this world, one that gives meaning and purpose as we journey along the road of life to our final destination.

Maurice Hogan SSC
St Columban's
Navan, Ireland

ACKNOWLEDGEMENTS

I owe a debt of gratitude to numerous biblical scholars without whom this book could not have been written. In particular, I wish to thank Professors Eric Voegelin and Brendan Purcell who opened up for me a whole new vista in biblical scholarship. I am also grateful to Archbishop Michael Neary who graciously consented to write the Foreword and to my Columban colleagues, Frs John Marley, Joe Houston, Tom O'Reilly and Michael Mohally, and Ms Caroline Hu who read the manuscript and offered valuable suggestions. Finally, thanks to the staff at Veritas for their courtesy and professionalism.

INTRODUCTION

It seems that Western culture is in need of revitalisation. For this to happen, though, we must first see the world and human beings as they *really* are. Humanity's self-understanding, which had been taken for granted for centuries past, has been badly obscured by modern ideologies. So much so that today this understanding is in danger of receding completely from view. Humans are in danger of becoming a raw material for experimentation and manipulation. Their transcendent end has been replaced by an inner-worldly fulfilment in a utopian future. That is why it can no longer be assumed that human beings, by themselves, are capable of providing their own moral and political order. The idea of a secular world, from which God is systematically excluded to make way for autonomous self-determination, is being called into question. That human beings are the self-sufficient ground of their own existence can no longer be taken for granted.

All of this is the result of a denial of objective truth about human beings which is founded on God, the Creator of the world, and in the very nature of reality itself manifest in human consciousness. When God and objective truth are denied, power, control and pleasure become the supreme values.

> Faith in modern man's omnipotence is wearing thin ... More and more people are beginning to realise that 'the modern experiment' has failed ... Man has closed the gates of heaven against himself and tried with immense energy and ingenuity to confine himself to earth. He is now discovering that ... a refusal to reach for heaven means an involuntary descent into hell.[1]

An Impoverished Vision

Ideologies such as secularism (that human beings are the exclusive agents of their own well-being and happiness), which is widespread today, arose from a false divinisation of human nature and can only be overcome through a re-discovery of the path to our true divinisation in the Judeo-Christian experience of order. All ideologies have in common a conscious revolt against the transcendent, divine ground of existence we call God and the construction of counter-grounds which Eric Voegelin calls 'second realities', that is, dream worlds created by people in a state of alienation from reality. The experience of attraction towards the divine ground of being, which is part of human experience, is deliberately excluded. Consciousness is then restricted exclusively to experiences in the material world.

This conscious limitation, according to Voegelin, breeds a preoccupation with power so that humanity becomes the end of its own existence. What is then revealed is the will to power, *libido dominandi* (lust for power, control), which is rooted in a hatred of reality and revolt against its Creator. All modern '-isms' have to do with the will to permanently transform the human condition. The exercise of power is capable of providing its own rationale and nothing is allowed to stand in the way of the pursuit of an era of universal happiness. This final state of perfection and resulting happiness will be achieved through an abundance of material goods and technological innovation. The transcendent God will be replaced by the New Man in a New World Order. This spiritual disease can affect an entire civilisation.

> Ideology is existence in rebellion against God and man. It is the violation of the first and tenth commandments, if we want to use the language of the Israelite order; it is the *nosos*, the disease of the spirit, if we want to use the language of Aeschylus and Plato. ... the search for truth concerning the order of being cannot be conducted without diagnosing the modes of existence in untruth. The truth of order has to be gained and regained in the perpetual struggle against the fall from it; and the movement towards truth starts from a man's awareness of his existence in untruth.[2]

What is rejected is reality; namely, that the world contains an intelligible order that is given to us for our good by a loving Creator, an order that can be discovered by the human mind. This was the achievement of Greek philosophy. Revelation, on the other hand, contains an account of actual events rooted in an existing transcendent order. It is not sceptical about the existence of an ordered objective world that can instruct us about 'what is'. Despite this, countries that have been proudly Christian for centuries, like Ireland, have suddenly decided to discard their traditions to join the secular world. And this notwithstanding the fact that the Christian faith is what best explains human meaning, dignity and destiny. For human beings cannot live long in a materialist, relativist, politically correct world ruled by 'the dictatorship of relativism'.[3] It is hardly surprising, then, that with the spread of relativism we find nihilism and despair on the one hand, and, on the other, a blind certainty offered by ideologies that claim to have answers to everything. Nevertheless, the hope that things will keep getting better seems to be fading in the face of economic crashes, political crises, the rise of global terrorism and the recent pandemic which laid bare for all to see the vulnerability and helplessness of human beings in the face of the unexpected. That is why the post-modern world is slowly coming to recognise the pressing need to recover the full truth of our humanity, its origin and destiny, that will guide us in living a fuller life more in accord with our true dignity as human beings created in the image and likeness of God: 'Reason needs to listen to the great religious traditions if it does not wish to become deaf, blind and mute concerning the essential elements of human existence.'[4]

A Richer Vision

We require a fuller vision of the dignity of persons, one that is solidly grounded in objective reality.[5] The human heart seeks meaning and purpose in life, one that leads to an intuition of transcendence and a desire for a relationship with the absolute we call God. Heart and head work together to make human beings come alive and reveal a more complete vision of the human person that in turn leads to true happiness. For every human being seeks happiness and all our choices in fact are in function of making us happy. The basic issues of life and death are not among those which progress in the sciences and technology can clarify. There is a set of human questions where the wisdom of the religious traditions is of central importance; for example, only the resurrection of Jesus brings true hope. But this hope in no way softens the reality of death. The risen Christ gives us the hope that, by God's grace, the entire person will be raised again to newness of life.

The view we have of happiness in turn is the key to all our major decisions and the direction of our lives. If happiness is the fulfilment of desire, then we must discover what our major desires are, what it is that drives us on, what we long for and seek fulfilment in. It seems that we are made for transcendent happiness, and when this is ignored there is a feeling of emptiness and loneliness which gives rise to feelings of depression and alienation. The error of today's materialistic culture is one of omission – ignoring indications of transcendence for which there is unmistakable evidence both from experience and human reason. We need to discard the veil of superficiality imposed on us through the media and popular culture so that we can see the true mystery of our being and the higher purpose and destiny to which we are called.

Otherwise, if we do not acknowledge our desire for transcendence, we are left with unfulfilled 'restless hearts'. The characteristic effect of this ignorance of God is, according to St Paul, enslavement to the 'elemental principles of this world' (Gal 4:8–9), with which one enters into a kind of relationship that soon turns into servitude because it rests on untruth. Paul develops his thought further in Romans 1:18–32, concerning which Joseph Ratzinger has this to say:

> In speaking of the philosophy of the heathens and its relationship to the existing religions, he [Paul] notes that the Mediterranean nations have reduced the knowledge of God to mere theory and, by reason of this perversion, have themselves fallen into perversity; by excluding from their way of life the foundation of all things, whom they very well know, they have distorted reality and have become disoriented, without norms and incapable of distinguishing what is base from what is noble, what is great from what is ordinary, and are thus, in practice, susceptible to every perversity – a train of thought to which we cannot deny a certain validity for the present as well.[6]

Introduction

☙

That God really does care and is loving was made explicit in God's self-revelation in the Old and New Testaments. Jesus Christ reveals the heart of God in his teachings, miracles, healings but especially in his suffering and death as an act of self-sacrificial love for us human beings. If love is central to the meaning of life, human dignity and destiny, then Jesus provides the fullest possible answer. God's unconditional love is now mediated through the Church founded by Jesus in its preaching, sacraments, worship and service to help us grow in faith, hope and love. Christianity can therefore become the source of the most pervasive, enduring and deep happiness and purpose in life. It fulfils our transcendent desires and spiritual and sacred intuitions. Otherwise, we will settle for this world alone, and undervalue our life, dignity and destiny.

A return to biblical revelation, not as a revival of a dead past but as a *living truth*, will provide an antidote to modern illusions of self-perfection. The experience of participation in the order of reality which is found in the symbolism of the Old and New Testaments is an essential part of that living spiritual truth which is necessary to confront the chaos of everyday life. In this way, the experience that underlies the biblical symbolism can again become a living reality in our day. An openness to transcendence must replace what Voegelin calls the ideological 'eclipse of reality'. This openness is preserved for us in the Bible which represents the experiences and their articulations by our predecessors in the faith in their search for the truth of existence.

In the Old Testament, the people of Israel broke free from the surrounding cosmological civilisations – the result of an 'irruption' of the divine beginning with Abraham. A new kind of people in history was created at the time of Moses. Throughout the Old Testament period there was continuous tension between life lived in obedience to the transcendent God revealed at Sinai and the organisation of a people for existence in the world that presented temptations to rebellion in the form of idolatry. In Christianity, what was going on in Israel was brought to clarity and fulfilment. Jesus Christ becomes the centre of history and the measure of what it is to be human. A new quality of life in the community of the Church with its goal in transcendent fulfilment beyond history becomes a possibility capable of realisation. The hope of Christianity is ultimately based simply on the fact that it tells the truth about life and death.

Accordingly, after a preliminary chapter that sets the context for a study of the biblical symbolism, we will inquire into the biblical anthropological vision in Genesis 1–11 that differentiates the God–human *relationship*. We will then survey the development of the God–human *experience* in Israel which underpins that relationship from the time of the Patriarchs. Christianity, the climax of revelation, is now set within the larger context of humanity's advance in consciousness and self-understanding. What is being attempted here is a retrieval of the meaning of human existence by exploring the content of experiences expressed through the biblical symbolism. These are the result of the questioning unrest and the desire to know on the part of humans on the one hand and of an 'irruption' of the divine that we call revelation on the other.

Endnotes

1   E.F. Schumacher, *A Guide for the Perplexed*, New York: Harper and Row, 1977, quoted in David Ehrenfeld, *The Arrogance of Humanism,* Oxford: Oxford University Press, 1981, p. ix.

2   Eric Voegelin, *Order and History, Volume 1: Israel and Revelation (The Collected Works of Eric Voegelin, Volume 14)*, Columbia, MI: University of Missouri Press, 2001, p. 24.

3   Joseph Ratzinger, Homily at Mass for the Election of a Pope, Vatican Basilica, 18 April 2005. https://www.vatican.va/gpII/documents/homily-pro-eligendo-pontif-ice_20050418_en.html; accessed on 12 November 2021.

4   Joseph Ratzinger, *Truth and Tolerance*, San Francisco: Ignatius Press, 2004, p. 252.

5   Robert Spitzer, Robin A. Bernhoft and Camille E. de Blasi, *Healing the Culture: A Commonsense Philosophy of Happiness, Freedom and the Life Issues*, San Francisco: Ignatius Press, 2000, pp. 35–117.

6   Joseph Ratzinger, *Principles of Catholic Theology*, San Francisco: Ignatius Press, 1987, p. 68.

CHAPTER ONE:
PARTICIPATION IN REALITY[1]

When we ignore the past, we deprive ourselves of the practical wisdom that guided our ancestors in previous generations. The accumulated wisdom of the past has something important to tell us. All cultures in fact have created stories to help people come to terms with the chaos that is part of living and which they must face. Chaos (the unpredictable) and order (the predictable) are the most fundamental elements of lived experience, but they are not like things or objects in the material world.[2] We have to deal and cope with these realities, not merely try to understand them. Every situation is made up of order and chaos, control and disorder. This is where the meaning of life is to be found. Stories have survived throughout the centuries because they provide guidance in dealing with the mystery of life and death. In these stories, truths are incorporated into the drama of existence that is portrayed, the basic elements of which are order and chaos. Because human beings are mortal and so vulnerable, suffering, pain and anxiety are an integral part of human experience. There is the fragility of life, the challenge of existence and the sense of despair evoked by the prospect of death. Reality as we experience it is not reducible to the material and objective alone, for we are actors, not spectators, in the drama of existence. What we subjectively experience is best described in story or narrative form.

Experience

We human beings are forever seekers after knowledge in order to make sense of our existence. Despite all the good things we have and enjoy, something inside us makes us forever restless, dissatisfied, frustrated and lonely. We desire so much and we are never completely happy with what we have. It is this desire that drives us to reach out beyond ourselves and spurs us on to action. But how do we channel this desire? How do we discipline it so that it leads to happiness and not frustration? We also long for love, companionship, community, friendship and affection, and these in turn lead us to ask fundamental questions about ourselves. In fact, human beings have always been asking questions like: Who and what are we? Where have we come from? Where are we going? What is the meaning and purpose of our life? How ought we to live? What is the meaning of evil, suffering and death? Is there life after death? Does God exist and, if so, what kind of God?

Truths about the human condition have been discovered from lived experience and have been handed on and articulated by gifted individuals in the form of narratives and dialogues, for example stories about the origin of the world and human beings. Although the basic questions regarding life remain the same, the way life is experienced, understood and expressed differs from one time, place and culture to another. Ancient societies like the Mesopotamian, Egyptian, Chinese and Indian civilisations expressed their manner of existence in narrative form called cosmological myth. The myth revealed the unfolding of their experiences which were articulated in the symbolisation of a political order through analogy with the cosmic order. The political order reflected the cosmic order, dispensing a just order of society through the king or emperor. One order was regarded as embracing the world and society, an expression of participation in reality that was compact, that is, the partners in being (God/gods and human beings, world and society) were as yet undifferentiated and the relationship between them not yet noticed. Greek philosophy and the Judeo-Christian religions offer more advanced and differentiated expressions of their self-understandings from insights gained during the course of their histories.

It takes only a little reflection to realise that there is something mysterious about the world which we inhabit, and this gives rise to a sense of wonder. There is also the human experience of not being self-sufficient, of finiteness, of creatureliness, of being born and bound to die, of dissatisfaction with the world that we experience as imperfect, of longing for perfection, happiness, meaning and the truth about life. This sense of wonder and questioning gives rise to seeking, searching, unrest and a desire to discover. There is also the experience of being moved, pulled or drawn to ask questions, as well as the counter-pull of the passions like pride, lust, anger, etc. This questioning unrest gives rise to a search for truth and meaning to escape ignorance by acquiring knowledge about how to live and cope with reality. Furthermore, human beings experience existence as contingent and have an intuition that ultimate happiness is not to be found in this world but above and beyond it. The great religious traditions see life as a divine gift and this gives rise to a movement of self-transcendence, an attempt to reach outside, above and beyond to make contact with the divine Being, the source of life. History, then, is not only a sequence of events in the rise and fall of civilisations and empires, but also the ever-expanding consciousness that we humans live and move and have our being in God, and that this is true for all peoples, at all times, and in all places.

Participation

The basic human experience is that of participation in reality. We experience ourselves as finite beings who are mere participants, part of a larger whole we call reality. The scope of this field in which we share is the community of God (gods) and human beings, world and society. We human beings want to explore this field to ascertain the true nature of these partners in the community of being as well as the relations between them. Since we are not self-contained entities, we are unable to assume the role of spectators vis-à-vis the rest of reality. We are more like actors in the drama of existence, but unlike actors in real life, we do not know the plot of this drama or indeed our own specific role in it. That is why we want to find out who and what we are, what we are meant to be, to do and to become. We look for the meaning of life, of suffering, evil and death. We want to know what kind of God created us since we are aware that we are not self-sufficient beings but that we owe our existence to another. This anxiety engenders an existential search for order and meaning in human existence which can never be total but has rather the character of a perspective. Our participation in reality, then, is not blind but is illumined by consciousness that enables us to explore reality. Gifted individuals have articulated their experiences of reality using language symbols. That is why experiences narrated in the Bible can illuminate our search for understanding as well. When we examine the biblical symbolism, we discover a historical process of experience and symbolisation that becomes more and more refined to give a better understanding of the world and of our place in it.

The human experience of participation in reality is sensed as a movement towards the divine ground of being (God) that arises from human existence in a state of unrest. This unrest is the result of experiences in a precarious existence in the 'in-between' – between the limits of birth and death, limitation and fulness, imperfection and perfection, mortality and immortality, order and disorder, truth and untruth. These experiences create a certain tension within us because, as well as seeking, we *feel drawn* to a more perfect existence. By using our reason we become conscious of existing from a ground outside ourselves and endeavour to order our existence by the insights we have gained. We discover that human existence has a dimension 'beyond', a direction illumined by consciousness that we call transcendence. History at its deepest level may then be understood as humanity's gradual opening to the transcendent dimension of its existence. The human condition as we experience it means living within the desire for perfection and the limitations that confine us.

The basic change in human existence is from life to death, which has from ancient times been accompanied by rituals celebrating the belief that humans exist beyond death. Refusal to accept death as final gave rise to attunement to what is more lasting by means of elaborate burial rituals in the belief that the human being must continue to exist in some manner beyond death. Attunement to the more lasting elements of reality – society, cosmos, the gods (God) – expresses the desire of overcoming death by being associated with realities that outlast the human lifespan. Human burials also expressed the desire of overcoming death by means of body adornments and grave goods that suggest a ritual to help the deceased navigate or negotiate the spirit world.

Consciousness

Human consciousness has a bipolar structure. We are capable of focusing both on things in the spatio-temporal world outside of us which are given in sense and on the ground of being which is beyond the world. Both experiences are articulated in language symbols. Consciousness develops as we focus on the world through our senses to gain knowledge of the external, material world. It can also be enriched when we focus on the unseen and mysterious spiritual world, on God the Creator, which results in clarity or lucidity, enlightenment or luminosity, as well as self-awareness. Hence, human beings can focus on both mundane and transcendent realities. Gifted individuals throughout history have given us insights into both the mundane world (e.g. scientists) and the transcendent world (e.g. philosophers, prophets, sages, saints, mystics).

> The order of history emerges from the history of order. Every society is burdened with the task, under its concrete conditions, of creating an order that will endow the fact of its existence with meaning in terms of ends divine and human.[3]

Experiences of transcendence that originated in Judeo-Christianity are narrated in the Bible, the result of revelation. From the perspective of spiritual vision we can speak of revelation in Israel when the transcendent God revealed himself beginning with the call of Abraham. Insight into the order of existence in the world became articulate during the course of Israelite history from the time of Moses and the Sinai experience, which grounded the identity of a people in its understanding of revelatory events. These are genuine experiences that are open to empirical analysis. Consequently, a realistic anthropology must be able to treat the phenomenon of revelation since it represents a decisive advance in human self-understanding. As a matter of historical fact, the maximum differentiation of the realms of being (God and human beings, world and society) was fully accomplished only within the realm of Christian experience. To provide an adequate understanding of human nature, therefore, a study of Judeo-Christian revelation is required. The experiences underlying biblical symbolisation need to be recovered and *re-enacted* by those who wish to seek and live the truth in their existence. The task of remembering is essential if we are not to lose the thread binding us to the sources of our civilisation. Otherwise there is a danger of losing our humanity.

Symbolisation

A study of the history of the biblical symbolism and its underlying experiences will deepen our understanding of human beings, their relationship to the world, society and God as well as an understanding of their own limitations. This existence in truth may be defined as a consciousness of the fundamental structure of existence together with a willingness to accept it as the human condition. The biblical symbolism also helps in the growth of human understanding as a response to the gradual unfolding revelation of God whose invisible divine presence is experienced as a movement in the soul of human beings everywhere throughout history. Revelation as expressed in the biblical record is the symbolic expression of wondering at, searching for and being drawn towards the divine ground of existence we call God. We are moving among symbols concerning the truth of existence which represent the experience of those who went before us. Symbols, unlike concepts, suggest rather than define and point to the unseen, though real, aspects of reality. Our search for meaning and understanding of our humanity, accordingly, is not conducted in a vacuum since the biblical symbolism itself was engendered by the experience of participation in reality, the result of individual human beings' experience of wondering, seeking, questioning and being drawn towards the divine ground of existence.

No other literature has recorded the gradual ascent to a more differentiated historical consciousness than the Old Testament symbolism, the result of an 'irruption' of the divine beginning with Abraham and later in the call of Moses who led Israel out of slavery to freedom. The Sinai covenant created a new kind of people who lived in history in the Promised Land but with a goal beyond history that was dimly perceived at first. During the course of its history opportunities for derailment occurred when society under the monarchy became too identified with its pragmatic history.

The spiritual development of the people was then taken up by the prophets who became the new spiritual leaders. This advancement was broadened by the wisdom teachers in the post-exilic period who concentrated on problems of daily living, while the psalms articulated the lived faith experience of the faithful remnant as they waited in hope for the coming of the ideal leader, the Messiah. Throughout the whole Old Testament period there was continuous tension between life in obedience to the transcendent God and the social and political organisation of a people for existence in the world. The root cause of this tension in the God–Israel *relationship* is articulated in Genesis 1–11. After a consideration of this material we will trace the development of the God–Israel *experience* from the time of the Patriarchs to the threshold of the New Testament era that gradually deepened this relationship.

In the New Testament, what was going ahead in Israel was brought to greater clarity and fulfilment. With the advent of Jesus Christ in history as *Logos* (word, meaning, reason), there was a gracious turning of God towards humanity. Christianity, then, can be located within the context of humanity's consciousness as it was illumined historically. Christ may be regarded as representing the high point of humanity's advance in spirit. He becomes the new Adam – humanity as God intended it to be, the centre of history, and it is possible to discover him through the symbolisation of the Christ-event recorded in the gospels. As the way, the truth and the life, Christ becomes the measure of human beings. The Pauline correspondence illustrates how human beings can be assimilated to Christ. A new quality of life in the 'in-between' based on love becomes possible in the community called Church that has for its goal complete union with God in a life after death.

Revelation contained in the Bible, therefore, becomes part of the larger context of human experience that begins with participation in reality and gives rise to a sense of wonder, of questioning, of the consciousness of seeking and being drawn beyond the present. The source of these movements is now revealed as the presence of a loving God who, though unseen in our world, keeps prompting us in our search while drawing us to himself. The biblical narrative gives an insight into God's working in our world, a luminosity that results in a clearer idea of where we have come from, where we are going and how to get there. This is now available to all who are open to receiving the Good News preached and witnessed to in the Church which is of its nature missionary. The Good News of Jesus Christ illuminates the mystery of our existence by giving a note of hope and joy in that we do not have to bear the burden of existence all by ourselves. The meaning of history at its deepest level then is that of a divine presence which gradually becomes more and more luminous in human consciousness and is expressed in symbolic language in the biblical record. It reveals the presence of a hidden God who is with us throughout our historical pilgrimage to guide us towards our destiny.

How do we make contact with the biblical God who created the world and is active in it? We encounter God by paying attention to our experience. Reflection on our experience reveals that the mysterious presence of God is possible because experience has a religious dimension to those who are open to it. We are usually only intermittently, if at all, aware of this presence because of our creatureliness and fears which resist the drawing love of God. In the Bible, people are said to have spoken with God, to have heard God. This is the only way they can speak of experiencing God, by using concrete, interpersonal language. There is nothing esoteric, mystical or ecstatic about it. People usually encounter God personally, though mediately, through a historical medium, for example by an imaginative and contemplative reading of the Bible or of nature. Like the disciples on the road to Emmaus, reflection on their experience will reinforce their belief: 'Did not our hearts burn within us as he talked to us on the road and explained the scriptures to us?' (Lk 24:32).

Belief in the real God comes through the community of people we call the Church. It also leads us to develop a relationship with Jesus so that we can follow him more closely as the way, the truth and the life (Jn 14:6) to lead us to God. This community helps us to shed false images of God previously formed and to overcome our fears. To motivate our actions and to be in tune with what God intends for us, our feelings need to be in touch with reality as well. The present, and nowhere else, is the place to discover what God wills for our future. We attune our actions to the Spirit who is present in our hearts (Rm 5:5) and reveals the love of God to us by interceding on our behalf (Rm 8:26–27).

Endnotes

1   For a more in-depth study, see Eric Voegelin, *Order and History, vol. 1: Israel and Revelation (The Collected Works of Eric Voegelin, vol. 14)*, (M. Hogan, ed.), Columbia: University of Missouri Press, 2001, pp. 39–50. See also, Brendan Purcell, *From Big Bang to Big Mystery: Human Origins in the Light of Creation and Evolution*, Dublin: Veritas, 2011, pp. 207–239.

2   Jordan B. Peterson, *12 Rules for Life: An Antidote to Chaos*, London: Penguin Random House UK, 2019, pp. xxvii–xxxv.

3   Voegelin, *Israel and Revelation*, p. 19.

CHAPTER TWO:
PRIMEVAL HISTORY (GENESIS 1–11),
PART ONE

Overview[1]

As a narrative, Genesis 1–11 forms a whole in which each individual section has its own contribution to make concerning God and human beings, world and society. It provides an answer to the mystery of the world that provokes awe and wonder as well as the search for answers. The story of primeval events is a relatively self-contained unity and a relatively late component of the Pentateuch. It deals with the universal, includes all humanity and has much in common with similar stories the world over. They all share a common interest in the origin of the present state of our world together with its inhabitants. It would be wrong, however, to see in Genesis 1–11 a sequence of events that are continued in Genesis 12. It is rather a series of happenings, embedded in genealogies which intends to present created being with all its basic characteristics. The primeval narrative articulates experiences which are common to humankind – creatureliness, limitation, sin, guilt, revolt – as well as human achievements and culture that belong to human existence as such. Human beings are oriented towards the mundane world – it is there that everything takes place concerning God's dealings with them.

The opening chapters of Genesis, then, are a record of religious experience, not a scientific description of the world. Rather, it portrays profound realities in a way that is graspable by human beings. For example, the purpose of Genesis 1 is to say one thing – that God created the world which comes from God's reason through his word. The theme of creation accompanied Israel throughout its history. Israel always believed in a Creator God, something shared with the greater civilisations that surrounded her. The creation theme became important during the Exile when Genesis 1–11 began to assume its final form, based on ancient traditions. Israel had lost its land and Temple. Had God abandoned them? The prophets of the Exile opened up a new phase by proclaiming that the God who had made promises to Abraham and led his people out of Egypt was not a god of one place, but the Creator and Lord of heaven and earth and the source of all that exists (Is 40:12–31).

Israel's creation faith was formulated over against the seemingly victorious religion of Babylon with its own creation account (*Enuma Elish*). The narrative assumes the cosmology of the time and its contents are distributed in a chronological arrangement extended over a week. It asserts that God alone created the world. In saying so, it rejected all the pagan myths, for example, by stating that the sun and moon are mere creatures, not gods, hung by God in the firmament to measure time and indicate the liturgical seasons. In confronting the pagan myths, Genesis 1 also reveals that the world is not the result of a demonic contest but came to be by the word of God who is reason and love. In this way, it marks a breakthrough from the fears and anxieties that had oppressed Israel's pagan neighbours who felt the need to constantly appease the gods by sacrificing even their children. Genesis 1 is followed by Genesis 2, an earlier account of creation using other imagery. In the psalms and wisdom literature, the movement to clarify faith in creation is carried further (Prov 8:22–31; Sir 42:15–43:33; Ps 104). The Old Testament creation accounts lead to Jesus Christ and the New Testament where we find normative creation accounts (Jn 1:1–3; Col 1:15–20; Rm 8:18–25). Only when we attend to the Bible as a whole do we fully understand its truth.

The narratives we find in Genesis 1–11 are not factual accounts of the sort that a modern historian would demand. They are 'historical' in the sense that they plumb the depths of history's meaning to portray those fundamental experiences that are common to all human beings from the very beginning and for all time. Human beings have been and remain such as they are described – limited, sinful creatures in need of a saviour. God's saving intervention, beginning with Abraham and culminating in Jesus Christ, is bound up with the sin and revolt of humankind. The genealogies, on the other hand, present human beings as creatures that continue in time because of the blessing of the Creator and who are spread out across the earth (chs. 5, 10). Vast periods of time are passed over quickly by means of these genealogies and a few carefully chosen, illustrative stories about the existence of the human family and their social environment are recorded.

The weaving of the two strands – narratives and genealogies – acquired its own independent significance and so appropriate attention must be given to the synchronic dimension, that is, the final text itself, its dramatic structure and stylistic features. Interest in human beings – their potential and their limitations – dominates the text. Humans are created by God to be his counterparts; they have the potential for a relationship with God that includes freedom, responsibility and conscience, and they can be called to account for what they do. The dynamic power to grow and develop is the result of the commission to work that makes cultural achievements possible. In this way, the history of civilisation is anchored in the command of God and becomes an important feature of the history of humankind. Suffering, restrictions of various kinds and death are part of the limitations of concrete human living. They are connected with sin, which occurs in a variety of concrete ways. God, however, preserves human beings by means of his retributive punishment. They need God to restrict them *so that* they can remain human. God's seemingly punitive interventions are therefore at the service of human life.

The opening chapters of Genesis also link the beginning of the world to the call of Abraham in chapter twelve. Genealogies trace the long succession of centuries from Adam to Abraham and the gradual expansion of human beings over the inhabited world (chs. 5, 10) as well as giving a sense of continuity. The narratives, on the other hand, are concerned with creation, human achievements, sin and its consequences – that is, various ways in which human beings use their freedom or misuse it to revolt against their Creator. They deal with individuals, groups or the whole of humanity. As preface to the call of Abraham, the Exodus and the history of Israel, they serve to answer questions as to why these events were necessary in the first place. The Saviour of Israel has now become the Creator and Lord of the world and of humankind.

Priestly Account

The priestly author opens the book of Genesis with his story of creation (Gn 1:1–2:4a) which is best described as a reflection, a meditation in rhythmic prose that asserts in an orderly and systematic fashion the creation of all that exists, including human beings, by God. Seven times it underlines the goodness of all creation. Planned as a whole, and so to be grasped as a whole, it is characterised by an onward, irresistible and majestic flow, solemn and rhythmic with repeated formulae (e.g. 1:3–5) and schematic speech. Everything is fitted into the pattern of a seven-day week – eight works in six days, two each on the third and sixth days. Creation is then described as a movement from chaos to an ordered world in which life exists. The verb 'to create' (*bara*) is given prominence in the title and is used three times in the creation of humans. The verbs employed point to the creation of a world as a suitable living space for human beings to inhabit. This world comes from God who created and put order into it and is ruled by space and time. The Creator is above and beyond the world (transcendent) and speaks and acts with sovereign freedom.

With the opening words, 'In the beginning, God created the heavens and the earth,' the author wishes to communicate that it is God who created everything that is in the world and, consequently, the total dependence of all on God. The world came into existence through God's word (*dabar*), a power that evokes structures in reality by naming them. In describing the manner of creation by word and in the order brought into existence by that word, the author wishes to communicate that the truth of the universe is not the result of chance, but of intelligence, freedom and beauty (*tob meod*, 1:31) that is identical with love. It begins with a precosmic description: the earth was formless and void (*tohu wa bohu*) that suggests by alliteration disorder, aimlessness and negativity. A second element (*tehom*) signifies the mass of aquatic chaos that enclosed the earth and enveloped it in darkness. A third element is the divine wind or spirit (*ruah*) that sweeps over the face of the waters. All three connote unformed chaos without life, uninhabitable by human beings. Creation then is regarded as the passage from chaos to an ordered world in which there is life, the result of God's word and action. God creates a universe in which life is found and which human beings inhabit. The various elements that make up the world are not an emanation of the divine substance, but the result of the personal will of God. God transcends his creation; creation belongs to God.

There is a progression from the world to what is in the world and upon the earth, from inanimate to animate, culminating in the creation of human beings. Everything begins with the Creator; all the rest are creatures. Even the sun, moon and stars, worshipped as gods in the neighbouring cultures, are mere creatures functioning for humans' benefit. This is the framework that links history to the beginning of time and space, the world and the human race. It is ordered and established by God and cannot be altered. The climax of the account is the seventh day, the holy day, the Sabbath that is blessed by God, thereby making it fruitful for human existence. It is a day in which human beings cease from work to enter into a relationship with the source of life in worship, praise and thanksgiving. The account is portrayed in such a way that human beings become conscious of how mysterious, incomprehensible and indescribable is the subject matter that is being narrated – the mystery of the universe. And yet, the priestly author is not aware of any opposition between a scientific and a theological explanation. On the contrary, by stripping the heavenly bodies and the earth of any form of divinisation, he makes the universe accessible to human research.

The creation of human beings is described in Genesis 1:26–29, the second work on the sixth day. This description stands out because of its length and the solemnity of its introduction, and the attention of the reader is focused by repetition. The creation of human beings is presented as the final and climactic act, the crown of creation. 'Let *us* make ...' is a rhetorical device to emphasise the solemnity and deliberativeness of this final act. *Adam*, though singular in form, is plural in content, as is evident from the plural form of the verbs and pronouns that follow. Consequently, humans do not exist in a sexless state, but as male and female (*zakar we-neqebah*), equal in dignity, called to communion and fruitfulness ('Be fruitful and multiply ...'), created as such by God and in accord with his design.

The symbols 'in our image [*selem*], according to our likeness [*demut*]', are practically synonymous and are used interchangeably elsewhere (Gn 5:1). They originate from sculptures or statues portraying human beings, usually kings or emperors. An image by its very nature points to something beyond itself and so implies a relationship with what it represents. There is a likeness or correspondence between a statue and the person it represents, and so a relationship is established between them. The essence of an image is that it represents something else; it goes beyond itself and manifests something that it itself is not. These symbols are used to suggest a relationship between God and human beings as well as an aptitude for it. Humans are created by God in such a way that a dialogue can take place between them. They are created in the divine image, and this characterises successive generations even after expulsion from the garden (5:3). It seems that God decided to create creatures who can somehow correspond to him, with whom he can have a relationship, that is, to whom he can speak and who can listen and respond ('... and he said to them', 1:28). This relationship is directed to the holy day (2:2–3) when worshippers hear God's word and respond to it in prayer. The author's understanding is that *all* human beings are created in this manner irrespective of race, colour or religion. It is true of all peoples, at all times, in all places. Accordingly, each person's uniqueness consists in being created in the image of God in his or her concrete existence. God can address each person as 'You' who in turn is an 'I' capable of entering into a relationship with God – one to whom God can speak and who can understand, respond and live in his presence.

The blessing of fertility ('Be fruitful...', v. 28) is the Creator's gift that makes the continuation of the human species possible in time and space (chs. 5, 10), in the succession and expansion of the human race made effective in begetting, birth and lifespan that makes the future possible. History grows out of this gift of procreation that God bestows on humans. They are also to exercise a benign sovereignty over creation by ruling over living creatures and subduing the earth. By their kingly exercise of authority (*radah*) over living creatures, and by cultivating the soil (*kabash*), they become stewards looking after the world as God's creation ('to till and keep it', Gn 2:15). No permission is given to exploit the environment for selfish purposes. Humans are to respect the environment and treat all living beings properly. In this way, a connection is forged between human beings and their environment. They are situated creatures living in the world, directed towards it, while the world is oriented towards humans to provide them with food and nourishment (v. 29). The whole project of the Creator is said to be 'very good' or beautiful, that is, suitable for the purpose or function for which it was created by God, namely, as a fitting home for humans to live out their lives and reach their destiny. Genesis 1 points to the wise design of the cosmos; it comes forth from God's mind through his word and finds its culmination in man and woman made in the image and likeness of the Creator to 'fill the earth' and to 'have dominion over it' as God's stewards (Gn 1:28).

This description highlights the fact that human beings can be properly understood only with reference to their Creator. Such a lofty concept of God and the process of creation itself adds a new dimension to human self-understanding and marks a new stage in a more advanced understanding of God and human beings, world and society. History then consists of both constants and variables – the succession of the generations and expansion over the earth that gives rise to different races, languages, epochs and cultures. But it is always essentially the same human beings who are creatures of God, called into a relationship with the one Creator. All peoples have the same dignity and character. Humans are also dependent creatures, called to trust in the God who created a good world for them to inhabit because of his goodness and love.

Human beings are by nature religious in that they are related to God, the source of life. This is true even when humans do not advert to it, try to suppress this desire or consciously deny it. The world is not corrupt, or evil, or demonic, nor is it the product of chance or necessity, but is declared to be 'good' and 'very good' by its Creator. The created world and human beings are creatures, distinct from but related to God and to each other. This adds a further dimension to human thought and marks a new stage in the history of religion that in turn gives rise to wondering, searching and questioning. Through all the variables of history, human beings are and remain God's creatures. The long lifespans in the genealogies (ch. 5) suggest the distant past that links it with the present and into the future. It is the same humanity throughout. Chapter ten details the expansion of humans over the known inhabited world. Seventy nations (denoting fulness) are mentioned, from which Abraham will descend (11:10–32). In this way, the story of Abraham, the people of Israel and the Church emerge from the general history of the human race and can be properly understood only within that context. They are part of the humanity created by God. This is the framework that links history to the beginning of time, the world and the human race. This history will extend to the people of God, to the coming of Christ, to the Church in our own day and into the future. This framework has been established by God, humans cannot change or alter it, although they may explore it.

According to the biblical author, God created human beings as male and female, i.e. as sexual beings. Consequently, sex plays an important role in human life. In Genesis, sex marks a sharp reaction to the cultures of the surrounding peoples. But sex is not just about sex, or procreation only. It has to do with life and what it means to be human, or rather human embodiment. The way we understand and express our sexuality reveals who we are as men and women, the meaning of love and the ordering of society. Love as the self-donation to another is already inscribed in the human body when we were created male and female and called to communion through the gift of self to another in the community called marriage. God created all things 'very good', including sex, but in our Western world there is often an under-evaluation of the body and sexuality. It is trivialised in a media that has forgotten the sacredness of the body which, by means of the sexual act, also symbolises the Creator's love for us. This comes about when one becomes a sincere gift to each other in a communion of persons in marriage. It is sexual attraction that leads to marriage and the family, the foundation of society, ethics and culture. Genesis calls us to reflect on the Creator's plan for us, inscribed in our bodies as male and female, as the basis for respecting the meaning and dignity of the human person created in God's image and likeness. We need to know the truth about sex in order to be set free to sincerely love another human being.

Yahwistic Narrative

The second creation narrative (2:4b–3:24) employs the genre of story that pays special attention to the creation of human beings, the relationship between the sexes and the meaning of human existence in its present existential state. Man and woman are joined together in joy and in pain. It also makes clear that it is only with the creation of man *and* woman that the project of creation is complete and the drama of life can begin. We are dealing here with a separate, composite narrative made up of two originally independent stories skilfully woven together (chs. 2, 3). The subject matter is human beings – their creation, relationships, transgression and consequences. After a lengthy introduction, the drama begins with God's word addressed to Adam (2:16–17), ascends to a climax with the disobeying of this command (3:6) and descends through the consequences of the transgression to expulsion from the garden which concludes the drama (3:23–24).

The setting which serves as a background to the creation of human beings is that of a desolate, uninhabited and uncultivated earth (2:5–6). God creates Adam out of the dust of the earth after the manner of a potter and makes him into a living person (*nefesh hayah*), which connotes movement, desire and orientation, for a human being is only a person in a living state. But life for the narrator is more than mere existence. By obeying God's word, human beings fashion a long and happy life when they choose life, not death (cf. 2:17). Created from the dust (*yasar*) suggests a frail, contingent, limited and mortal creature. Adam is placed in a garden that is fertile, luscious, rich in minerals and well watered. It is adorned with fruit-bearing trees 'pleasant to the sight and good for food' (2:9), including the tree of knowledge of good and evil which figures prominently in the narrative. The tree of life is a symbol rooted in human experience expressing a desire and search for immortality. It articulates the intuition of what human beings always have had, namely, that we are made for life, not for death. The image of a garden connotes a homely atmosphere that shelters, nourishes and sustains. Adam is placed in the garden 'to till it and keep it' (2:15), so work is part of what it means to be human. He is free to eat the produce of all the trees of the garden except one, and God's word (2:17) places before him the possibility of obedience and freedom of decision. No explanation is offered for this prohibition; it is part of creaturely existence to be limited and also free. It is one of those things that enables Adam to live with reference to God, for a relationship with God becomes possible only through his word. Adam is free to accept or reject this word, to say yes or no, to obey or disobey, with a warning of the consequences: '… for on the day you eat of it you shall most surely die' (v. 17). God's word then serves to give expression to the limits of that freedom enjoyed by human creatures. By rejecting God's word, human beings disconnect themselves from God. To say no to God is to say no to life, for life comes from God (2:7).

However, the man placed in the garden is not yet the completed creature God has in mind. He needs a helper as his partner. Sub-human living creatures are not suitable, but they still have a role to play when Adam names them, thereby assigning them a place and a meaning in his world. Only with the creation of woman, though, is God's project brought to completion. Humankind is man and woman, since it is not good for man to be alone. He needs a suitable partner ('ezer kenegdo, 'a helper fit for him', 2:18), one that connotes for the narrator mutual assistance, companionship and understanding. The man is cast into a deep sleep – he is not privy to the creation of woman, which is a mystery. The description of the formation of the woman is told in such a way that the very process itself explains how man and woman belong together and are attracted to each other (vv. 22–23). The woman is received with a song of joy. Human beings, then, exist as man and woman destined to be joined in a community of persons that includes the bodily and spiritual, mutual support and companionship. The man leaves his family to enter into a community of life that is characterised by concern, fidelity, affection as well as sexual union (dabaq). Becoming 'one flesh' (basar) connotes as well a complete personal communion in the love of man and woman for each other. In this way, the Creator's intention regarding their manner of living is brought to completion.

Chapter two is concerned with those relationships that make for a full, rich and happy human existence as persons. Human beings are related to God from whom they receive form and life. The description stresses the distance between them and the Creator, as well as the fragility of the human creature. At the same time, it also highlights God's concern and care when he places the man in a fertile garden to till and keep it. God's word confronts the man with a sense of responsibility, freedom of decision and the question of obedience to enable him to live concretely with reference to the reality of God. It is part of the very nature of being human to see oneself as a free being before the word of God which humans can obey or disobey when they succumb to temptation (3:1–7). The closeness of the relationship between the man and the woman is reflected in the description of the creation of the woman. She is called woman ('ishshah) after man ('ish) reflecting the deep bond between them. Adam also has a relationship with all other living creatures. By naming them, they are to serve him, thereby giving expression to his autonomy within creation. The relationship between Adam and the earth ('adam/'adamah) is evident in his creation from the earth as well as his commission to take care of it. Later, as a result of disobedience, this care will be accompanied by effort and toil, sweat and obstacles, until he returns to the earth at death (3:17–19). What then are human beings? Formed from the dust of the ground and destined to return to it is a way of saying that humans are limited yet fashioned by God from God's good earth. Despite every distinction that culture and history have brought about, all human beings are from the earth, they are the same; there is only one humanity. They are beings in relationship with God, with other human beings and with creation that is expressed concretely in gratitude, family life, society and work (in the economic, political, cultural and environmental spheres). In the world, humans are to cooperate with one another to construct a more humane world that is worthy of human dignity – a civilisation of love.

Chapter three reveals the sin which lay at the origins of humanity as the root cause of all moral evils with which history has been plagued. Together with chapter two it presents in narrative form the present state of humanity and how it came about. It begins with a temptation scene (3:1–7) consisting for the most part of a dialogue between the woman and the serpent (a fertility symbol in the surrounding cultures that posed an attraction for the Israelites), one of the cleverest ('arum) of the wild beasts and so a suitable candidate as tempter. Pagan fertility cults posed a permanent temptation to idolatry for Israel which caused them to abandon their covenant relationship with God. At the time the paradise story was reaching its final form there was the danger that Israel would succumb to the seductive elements of these religions (1 Kgs 18, Elijah's confrontation with idolatry). Through the fertility cults the serpent now speaks to the woman. The kernel of the temptation is the possibility of an extension of human existence beyond the limits set for it by God. This scene serves to reveal another aspect of human life, an unpleasant truth about human nature in its present condition.

With Israel's temptation in mind, the storyteller portrays the temptation of the first couple and consequently the nature of temptation and sin in every age. The serpent begins with an apparently reasonable enquiry but with an insinuation that God's intentions for his human creatures cannot be trusted. No explanation is offered for the serpent's presence because the temptation to overstep limits is part of the human condition as we experience it. The serpent calls into question God's prohibition, not by denying it, but by exaggeration ('any tree'), thereby sowing a doubt about God's intentions. The woman answers correctly but adds a slight refinement ('nor touch it'), thereby altering God's word as well. The serpent then goes on to propose a new dimension of life, the result of eating the forbidden fruit: 'You will not die … your eyes will be opened and you will be like God, knowing good and evil' (3:4–5). This is a particular way of knowing that results in becoming master of one's own existence. It is also a divine attribute (3:22) and linked to wisdom (*lehaskil*, 3:6) – that practical search for insight and understanding that will lead to success in life. The result would be an unbridled ability to fully control one's life without reference to God.

Temptation then is the possibility of an extension of human existence beyond the limits set by God at creation. It arises from interactions with the external world and an internal conversation in which alternatives are weighed before deciding. For as well as being tempted by the serpent, the woman is led astray by the desire of the senses – the fruit is attractive, enticing and useful. This desire is normal, perfectly human and God-given – humans are created with it. But when this desire finds itself before something that defines the Creator–creature relationship, then the woman must decide which alternative she wishes to embrace. For desire is ambivalent; it can elevate human life or put it in danger when it leads to a disturbance in the God–human relationship. When humans, in their aspiration for mastery and control of life, disobey God's word and overstep creaturely limits which protect their relationship with God, then they are no longer fully human because the relationship that guaranteed their full humanity has been severed.

The woman, nevertheless, decides to disobey out of an exaggerated sense of autonomy and is fully responsible for her decision. The man apparently goes along, conforms and, by allowing another person to decide for him, avoids a personal decision which is his alone as someone unique and responsible before God. Temptation, then, is something that begins from without, but finds a ready collaboration within a person that moves one to an over-evaluation of oneself and leads to blindness, error and bias in perceiving one's own reality in relation to God. Transgression is a renunciation of the truth because both the man and the woman chose to heed the voice of another rather than obey God's word; the woman by acting, the man by failure to act.

The result of their disobedience is that their eyes are opened to the pained realisation of altered conditions. Instead of becoming God-like, there is shame and fear of exposure which they try to conceal. They become self-conscious of their own vulnerability, and the disruption in their relationships is experienced as shame, fear, hiding and later on as scapegoating. God questions them to get them to realise what they have done and to acknowledge and accept responsibility for their actions. They are made aware that their action was taken in defiance of God which is the essence of sin: 'Is it that you have eaten from the tree from which I forbade you to eat?' (3:11). In doing so, God is showing his concern for his creatures, for, when he calls them to account, he is taking them seriously as persons. They have an opportunity to defend themselves, but instead, the man blames God for the woman God gave him, while the woman blames the serpent. But they are responsible for their actions that have resulted in a disruption in relationships – alienation from God (hiding), a fractured relationship between the man and the woman (scapegoating), and between humans and the environment (hardship).

Their sin brings about eventual expulsion from the garden as well as a variety of limitations that cause suffering. There is enmity and struggle between the serpent's and the woman's offspring that will affect their descendants. The woman will have pain in childbearing and will be subordinate to her husband, that is, there is tension and frustration between complementary and subordinate roles between man and woman, the result of sin. The woman still enjoys the dignity and joy of motherhood (3:20), but there will be pain and frustration in her life as well. The man's work from now on requires effort, sweat and toil in overcoming obstacles until he returns to the earth at the end of his life. Still, God's care and protection accompanies them as they are expelled from the garden (3:21), but they are prevented from eating from the tree of life to gain immortality and will eventually die.

The narrative paints a picture of life as we experience it, though not as God had originally intended. In their fallen state, human beings experience life as threatening and ambivalent. On the one hand, they are the recipients of God's blessing, protection and care; on the other, they experience limitations as creatures in the form of guilt, suffering, toil and eventually death. These are the consequences of the misuse of freedom. Genesis 2-3, then, is a narrative depicting the specifically human, recurring traits that are common to all people throughout history and are constant and enduring. The story tries to account for alienation from God, the experience of frustration in the living out of relationships and eventual death. This, however, is not the last word. There is alienation from God but not total separation. The couple are expelled from the garden, but God grants them life. They are still God's creatures, recipients of his care and protection. The life of work outside the garden will give meaning to their alienated existence.

What is portrayed is a realistic picture in narrative form of the present condition of humankind. Unlike the theory of evolution, it does not attempt to explain how humans developed biologically, but what they are in their existential situation – some basic truths about the present human condition, the result of overstepping creaturely limits by disobeying God's word. Taken together, Genesis 2–3 describes the present state of human beings with all their capabilities and limitations.

> We have regarded the creation narratives as an answer to the question 'whence', i.e., what is the origin of the world, of man? ... It is not the philosopher inquiring about his origins that spoke in the creation narratives; it was man threatened by his surroundings. The background was an existentialist, not an intellectual problem.[2]

Sin is a rejection of relationality because it wants to make human beings into gods. Since humans are relational beings, sin also touches others involved in the relationship. The narrative tells us that the network of human relationships has been damaged from the beginning. We are all from the first moment of our existence confronted with a sin-damaged world. We enter into a situation in which relationality has become flawed. From this predicament, human beings are unable to extricate themselves. The concept 'Original Sin' captures the fact that, basically, human history is a history of alienation that is contrary to human nature as envisaged by the Creator.

Since the relationship with the Creator has been damaged, only God himself can become our Saviour to re-establish the network of relationships that have suffered from alienation. The harmony between the Creator, humankind and the created world was disturbed by Adam and Eve, human beings, who wished to take the place of God and refused to acknowledge their creaturehood. As a result, the relationship between them became strained, the work of tilling and keeping the soil became disrupted and conflict arose between humans and the rest of creation (3:17–19). Once human beings, instead of acting as God's co-workers, set themselves up in place of God, they end up provoking a rebellion on the part of nature that is very much in evidence today. Their relationship with creation is an important element for the development of human identity and not even human sinfulness has eliminated their duty as guardians and stewards of the world.

The narrative attempts to explain human existence in its essential elements. The narrator presents in story form the constantly recurring traits that are specifically human, common to all peoples, in all places, at all times. These traits accompany human beings throughout their history. People are and remain such as they are described, and these traits also characterise the people with whom God relates throughout salvation history.

Implications

Desire and Limits

In the narrative of Genesis 2–3, something fundamental is being said about the human condition because humans do experience life in two contrasting ways.[3] On the one hand, they experience desire for something better, above and beyond their present experience. Humans are endowed with a strong desire for a better quality of life and knowledge in order to control and master life. This desire is natural and God-given. On the other hand, there are inescapable limits. Human beings cannot fulfil all their desires because certain things cannot be changed and must be accepted. As well, limits seem to encroach more and more with the passing of years through illness, tragedy, unfulfilled desires, old age and eventually death.

Furthermore, there is tension between desire and limits. This tension can be painful and cause suffering, so there is the temptation to eliminate it, for example, by overstepping creaturely limits to gain complete control of life in defiance of the will of the Creator. This comes about by succumbing to the illusion of being the sole guarantor of one's own well-being. But this results in a disturbance of the Creator–creature relationship, for humans exist only in a creaturely state and so are limited. To attempt to overcome limits is at the expense of truth about the human condition and usually at the expense of other people as well. When this is attempted, the human creature is endangered, and this will involve continual frustration when God thrusts humans back within their creaturely limits precisely to preserve their humanity. Another way to eliminate or ease the tension between desire and limits is the attempt to suppress desire (Buddhism). But it is inconceivable that a normal human being would be indifferent to the fulfilment of desire since all human activity, accomplishments and achievements are sustained by desire and aspiration of some kind or other.

Nevertheless, desire keeps pushing against limits in a search for something better and this aggravates the tension between them. Humans must come to terms with limits and this takes place in the very act of deciding. For as well as the good that is chosen, other good things are rejected. Human decision involves the exercise of freedom, yet, paradoxically, every decision ratifies our own limitations, and this is what makes deciding so difficult. Yet decide we must, for the alternative would be drifting through life without commitment of any sort, or allowing others to decide for us. Still, our highest dignity as human beings consists in freely deciding and accepting responsibility for what we do. What is important is that we choose well. God takes us seriously when he calls us to account for what we do or fail to do. Consequently, every advance in the direction of what claims to be superhuman, be it in politics, in the cultural sphere, in science, technology or medicine, endangers the truly human and so will involve a continuous frustration of any such tending to omnipotence.

To appreciate the full import of the narrative in Genesis 2–3, therefore, it is necessary to renounce a historicising mentality, because the narrative does not pretend to be a historical reconstruction of the life of the first man and woman. In it something important and enduring is being said about human beings in their concrete, existential state, with all their potentialities and limitations. While religious faith and hope offer a solution to the problems of living, they do not provide an exemption from having to face limits, decisions, suffering and death. Religious living retains a sober anchorage in the concrete realities of daily life when people find themselves challenged and put to the test by God, called to decide rather than be merely consoled and affirmed.

Marital Love

Something fundamental is also being said about the relationship between man and woman. Everybody instinctively knows that the tension, conflict and heartache in the male–female relationship that is widespread today is not normal. We suspect that something is wrong and we find an 'echo' of how things originally were meant to be through the symbolism of the biblical language in the early chapters of Genesis.[4] In Genesis 2, Adam alone is a person in a world of living creatures who has difficulty finding a suitable companion, for it is not good for man to be alone (2:18). Eventually, he achieves personal unity with another person like himself, but one who is different, and both are called to live in a loving communion in a union of persons. The biblical author tells us that both were naked and felt no shame (2:25). Shame is a symbol that functions as a self-defence against being treated as an object for sexual exploitation. After the couple succumb to the serpent's temptation by attempting to overstep their creaturely limits, they experience shame and proceed to clothe themselves as a protection against what has now become a disordered relationship (3:7). For it is only a person who is free from the compulsion to selfishly grasp, use and possess another person who is capable of being truly loving, of being a true gift to another person. This is the meaning and purpose of sexuality.

Man and woman are meant by the Creator to be a gift to each other in marriage which normally leads to fruitfulness in children. Fatherhood and motherhood crown and reveal the mystery of sexuality.

The opposite of this self-giving love is using another person as a means of self-gratification. But we also know that our hearts are deeper than this desire for self-gratification. That is why our hearts become the battleground between love (the free giving of oneself to another) and self-gratification (our disordered desire to grasp, use and possess another person for selfish pleasure). Sex has always and everywhere been regarded as something 'special'. That is why in all cultures the use of sex has been protected in some way – because it was regarded as connected with a sense of the 'sacred' and permissible only in marriage. Marriage includes fruitfulness ('Be fruitful and multiply') and faithfulness ('cleave to his wife … one flesh'). It is the human *person* who is involved in both.

Sexuality, therefore, as self-giving is properly realised in marriage and family life that includes respect, reverence, faithfulness and fruitfulness, rather than power, control or domination. It seems then that much of our modern world has lost sight of the greatness, dignity and purpose of human sexuality. There is a need to situate sex within a total vision of the human person as Genesis 1–3 suggests. What is involved is human life itself: its source is in sex, mediated through marriage and consummated in happiness. Marriage is a sacred institution that gives joy, mutual loving and new life, but also demands discipline. Humans need to practise self-control in order to be able to direct erotic desire to what is true, good and beautiful in marriage because the future of humanity passes by way of marriage and the family. Created male and female, possessing sexual desire and longing for communion with another human being are fundamental facts of life. Sex has been created by God as something good that is both life-giving and love-giving and so demands respect. The biblical authors call us to live the truth of being male and female. It is a very positive, joyful and hope-filled message, a real alternative to the trivialisation of sex seen everywhere today.

Endnotes

1   For much of this material, I am indebted to Claus Westermann, *Genesis 1–11: A Commentary,* London: SPCK, 1984.

2   Claus Westermann, 'Biblical Reflection of Creator-Creation,' in Bernhard W. Anderson (ed.), *Creation in the Old Testament,* Philadelphia: Fortress Press, 1984, p. 98.

3   Bartholomew M. Kiely, *Psychology and Moral Theology,* Rome: Gregorian University Press, pp. 173–194.

4   John Paul II, *Man and Woman He Created Them: A Theology of the Body,* Boston: Pauline Books and Media, 2006.

CHAPTER THREE:
PRIMEVAL HISTORY (GENESIS 1–11),
PART TWO

Fratricide

In Genesis chapters 4–11 we find stories that recount the progressive deformation of humankind. The story of Cain and Abel (4:1–16), offspring of Adam and Eve, is a narrative concerning two brothers at enmity with each other and follows the expulsion from the garden of the first couple. As well as disruption in the man–woman relationship, there is also disorder in the relationship between brothers – opposition, enmity, rivalry – by the very fact of their living together. The story serves to illustrate the further alienation of humans from God.

Because the Creator gave humans the commission to work (2:15), the natural consequence is the division of labour and the variety of work and occupation. When brothers live side by side with equal rights, inequality becomes a possibility. Conflict arises from the acceptance and non-acceptance by God of the offerings: one is accepted by God; the other is rejected and so inequality enters into community life. This is a story-teller's way of saying that there is inequality in social life that is mysterious and cannot be fully explained. This inequality is one of the main reasons for conflict between brothers, the result of envy and resentment that can lead to murder. Cain's reaction of envy is normal and justified because for no apparent reason he feels disadvantaged. It all depends on how he will respond. Cain is warned not to let sin become his master which he ignores (v. 7). The murder of Abel is followed by an untruth in which Cain tries to cover up his deed, but murder cannot be hidden from God and so Cain is cursed, driven out and condemned to a life of frustration. He becomes a displaced person exposed to the danger of death. Cain, the wanderer (*nad*), consumed by guilt, is condemned to settle in the land of restless life (*nod*), east of Eden where he lives a life of alienation from God. Nevertheless, God's continual protection accompanies him. It seems then that transgression of creaturely limits has social implications as well, for humankind is not just Adam and Eve, but also Cain and Abel who are part of society that includes different occupations. And so, there arises the possibility of inequality among brothers who will not accept their creaturely limitations.

The story of the first murderer and slayer of his brother which has roughly paralleled the story of the 'fall' in the preceding chapter has served the valuable purpose of showing how the way of the transgressor eventually has social implications and cannot be restricted to a private and personal offence against God alone. In the intention of the Yahwist, Cain is every bit as possible an everyman as were the man and the woman in the garden.[1]

The narrative deals with basic relationships in the human community. Living together as brothers is part of social existence as human beings who stand in a community relationship completely different from that of husband and wife. It includes inbuilt success and inequality in the different occupations which form the basis of all social life and inevitably lead to conflicts.

Ambiguity of Culture

Cain becomes the founder of a city which makes possible the beginnings of culture. Genesis 4:17–26 describes the founding of a city (architecture), the development of agriculture, music (arts), and metalwork (technology and weaponry). The division of labour leads to the development of culture. This is a story of progress, invention and discovery, the result of human beings' commission to work leading along the path that is the basis of civilisation. Nevertheless, this development conceals a danger in an exaggerated sense of power that is evident in the song of Lamech (vv. 23–24). His covetousness (bigamy), self-assertion and pride demand an exaggerated retribution for the slightest injury. In this is captured the ambivalence of progress. Although it opens up to a greater quality of life, pride and arrogance on the part of humans can lead to reckless revenge that causes social disruption. In 4:26 (Enosh), we are told that worship of God is determinative for the whole of human history. This comes about through invocation of the name of God.

Uncontrolled Passion

Following chapter five, which traces the succession of generations existing through time, Genesis 6:1–4 is another brief narrative woven out of fragments of myth that circulated in the ancient cultures. These fragments are employed to say something about the effects of uncontrolled passion. The 'sons of God' are so powerful that when they desire beautiful women, they can take them by force (polygamy). This conceals a danger of overstepping creaturely boundaries and God intervenes to set limits to the human lifespan. Human beings, it seems, are constantly trying to overstep the limits that separate them from God. The background to this enigmatic story is a patriarchal society in which powerful men can acquire beautiful women just because they are powerful (e.g. the affair of David and Bathsheba). So, human passion needs to be disciplined and controlled, otherwise there is a danger that disordered passion will lead to aggression by superior force in the human desire to achieve immortality through offspring. This story serves as a further illustration of increasing sinfulness, in this case the result of uncurbed passion. The bigamy of Lamech has now developed into polygamy. The result is social chaos and disorder and leads into the story of the Flood.

The Meaning of Love[2]

The love between man and woman was called *eros* by the Greeks. Used infrequently in the Old Testament, it was replaced by *agape* in the New Testament to highlight what is distinctive about Christian love. Nevertheless, from the Enlightenment (seventeenth century) onwards this new element was seen as something purely negative. It was said that *agape* poisoned *eros* (attraction between the sexes) so that now it had become a vice, and was reinforced by the Church's prohibitions. The Creator's gift of sexuality, the most precious thing in life, offers the possibility of happiness as a foretaste of heaven. But does Christianity in fact destroy *eros*?

In the pagan religions surrounding Israel, *eros* found expression in the fertility cults which included sacred prostitution as a means of achieving fellowship with the gods. The Israelite religion rejected this perversion as a destructive form of *eros* because it dehumanised people – temple prostitutes were being exploited as persons. If *eros* were to provide a foretaste of that happiness for which human beings yearn and not just passing pleasure, then it needed to be purified and disciplined, not suppressed. To treat *eros* properly, purification and growth in maturity are called for, including renunciation, if it is to be healed and restored to its true grandeur. The challenge of *eros* is overcome only when body and soul are in harmony, for it is not the spirit alone nor the body alone that loves. It is the whole person, composed of the union of body and soul, that allows *eros* to mature and attain its goal.

Christianity has also been criticised for being opposed to the body. In contemporary Western culture, *eros* is reduced to sex as a commodity and the body is used and exploited at will as a purely material entity. In this way, the body is debased, for it is no longer the expression of the whole person, but merely regarded as a biological object. Since Christianity regards human beings as a unity of body and spirit, if *eros* is to lead beyond the self, it calls for renunciation, purification and healing to move beyond self-seeking. Love then becomes concern and care for the other and is ready and willing to sacrifice for the sake of the other.

True love is a journey, an on-going exodus out of a closed, inward-looking self to liberation and freedom through self-giving to another human being. Jesus' path through the cross to resurrection demonstrates the essence of true love. Christian love, therefore, distinguishes *eros* (possessive love) and *agape* (self-sacrificing love) but the two can never be separated. At first, there is love as *eros* in being attracted to another person, but this becomes less and less concerned with the self and seeks rather the happiness of the other. In this way, *agape* enters into love. We must also be willing to receive love as a gift if we are to be a source of love for another. Christian love is, therefore, a single reality with two different dimensions. It is based on God's love for human beings, a love that is both passionate (*eros*) and sacrificial and forgiving (*agape*), as proclaimed by the prophets (Hos 11:1–9; Ez 16). *Eros* is directed to marriage and only in this way does it fulfil its deepest purpose. It then becomes an icon of the relationship between God and his people. God's way of loving, which is both passionate and sacrificial, becomes the measure of human love.

Corruption, Catastrophe, Restoration

The flood narrative (6:5–9:17) is a composite of two originally independent stories and this accounts for the inconsistencies and duplications we find therein. The narrator created out of both traditions a new, flowing narrative that deserves to be considered in the form it was given.

As the narrative begins, human wickedness has increased, and corruption has become widespread, leading to depravity and lawlessness (6:5–12). So great is the corruption, the narrator tells us, that God regretted having created humankind and now needed to intervene to protect his creation by ridding it of evil. Alone in the midst of sinful humanity is Noah, a man of integrity among his contemporaries. Noah and his sons are ordered to build an ark to save themselves and a representative sample of creatures from imminent catastrophe.

In a series of scenes, the narrative moves towards a climax and then descends towards a conclusion. It reaches a crescendo as the rising waters engulf the polluted earth and then follows a reverse pattern. With the coming of the flood and the rising waters the corrupt earth and its inhabitants are destroyed. Then, when all seems lost, God remembers Noah (8:1) and the waters recede, making a new beginning possible. There is the gradual drying up of the earth, the order of nature is restored, covenant blessings and peace symbolised by the rainbow are bestowed. Noah and the other creatures survive the catastrophe. God saves a faithful remnant.

The first group of scenes depicts the acts of divine justice that bring destruction upon the earth which has become filled with violence. It represents a movement towards chaos with the hero Noah and the remnant as survivors of the catastrophe. The second group shows the divine compassion that renews life upon the earth and represents a movement toward a new creation with Noah and his family as representatives of a new humanity that will inherit the earth. The rainbow is a sign and pledge of life for coming generations which signals the beginning of a new creation.

The author is less interested in describing the destructiveness of a flood than with raising the possibility that the human race could destroy itself through wickedness and corruption were it not for the intervention of God to preserve a remnant on account of the faithfulness of a few. Flood narratives worldwide were used to give expression to the experience of threats to human existence that also occur in tsunamis, hurricanes, earthquakes, pandemics, etc. Human beings instinctively know that they are creatures and that they cannot take for granted their existence in the world. This uncertainty gives rise to anxiety and a feeling of threat. There is the intuition that it is God, not humans, who holds the world in his hands and is the source of its stability. Human beings are contingent creatures, and this realisation leads to uncertainty, anxiety and threat. The flood story then serves to articulate an awareness of finitude and sinfulness. God holds humans accountable for their misdeeds yet saves a faithful remnant. He is both Judge and Saviour as well as Creator and Preserver. Sinful humans experience God's judgment, but also his favour. The flood is motivated by God wishing to cleanse his creation of corruption that had become widespread. In doing so, God is protecting humans from disaster so that humanity cleansed of corruption can begin anew. From now on, God guarantees to preserve the renewed order 'as long as the earth lasts' (8:22), even though humans resume their old pattern of disobedience.

The biblical narrative of destruction/salvation by the one God is expressing something fundamental for humanity and its understanding of existence. The pattern of degeneration, command to construct the ark, universal destruction reaching cosmic proportions, the salvation of a remnant, a new beginning in the rhythm of the seasons and God's providence in stabilising the world, shows that it is the Creator who upholds the world as humans experience it.

The story of the Flood, therefore, as recounted in the book of Genesis, is of profound importance as a landmark in the history of religion. The idea that human sinfulness finds its expression in the state of society, and that God holds men and society accountable for their misdeeds, is revolutionary in the ancient world.[3]

In the covenant with Noah, Israel recognises something akin to a cosmic reordering in the promise that it will be maintained (8:22) and so becomes a point of contact with the cosmological religions of humanity. It shows that there is a kernel of truth hidden in the mythical (cosmological) religions. There is the conviction that the cosmos and its myth, just like history, speak of God, the Creator, and can lead people to God. In Israel, for the first time ever, 'history' is perceived as a genuine reality not reducible to the cosmos and offers a different vision of an *active* God in whom the oppressed can put their hope.

Impiety towards Parents

Post-deluvial humanity makes a new beginning in the story of Noah and his sons (9:18–27) as well as illustrating yet another way in which humans try to transgress limits, this time by an act of impiety towards parents. The occasion is the drunkenness of Noah, which is linked to the cultivation of the vine, a step forward from agriculture that produces the necessities of life. The earth also yields a product that brings relaxation and joy to human living. However, over-indulgence in wine can weaken one's faculties resulting in nakedness which in Israel was regarded as the loss of human and social dignity. The episode also serves to illustrate what can happen between father and sons: Ham mocks Noah and is cursed and punished in a life of disgrace as a slave to his brothers; the other sons act with filial piety and are blessed. It is only when there is respect for the achievements of previous generations that progress, culture and values can be appreciated and passed on. The narrator has given us different examples of culpability in the basic communities of human relationships: man–woman; brother–brother; now parents–children. Here he is emphasising something that took the form of the fourth commandment of the Decalogue in Israel. Human community is healthy only where there is an attitude of respect between the older and younger generations. In this way, past achievements are preserved and make further progress possible.

Humanity in Revolt

The Babel narrative (11:1–9), like the flood story, concerns the whole of humanity – this time in its striving for fame and recognition. The boundaries of creaturehood are in danger of being breached in an attempt to reach the abode of God in the heavens symbolised by a tower 'with its top reaching heaven' (v. 4). The story is situated in Babylon, the cradle of civilisation. The building of a tower reaching the heavens, the abode of God, is seen as an aspiration to fame ('name') with the possibility of overstepping limits. Against such hubris that attempts to become like God, God acts to prevent a future danger, namely, the absolute autonomy of human beings that calls into question their creaturely status over the Creator. The impression given is that humankind is no longer satisfied with its limited state and wants to force its way into the heavenly realm in its desire for recognition and fame. The building of such a massive structure presupposes advanced technical skills, but also hides a possible risk. For it is only humans living within their creaturely limitations who can find fulfilment. Striving for fame, recognition, independence and control vis-à-vis the Creator disturbs the proper relationship between Creator and creature. Human cultural advancement and invention, while good in themselves, conceal a danger. God's intervention results in the alienation and confusion of the peoples who are no longer able to communicate among themselves. When each individual wants to become a god, that is, to determine one's own destiny solely by oneself, then other people become a threat and true communication becomes impossible. People need to be united inwardly so that they can also be united outwardly. The narrative here is an attempt to explain how the present situation came about.

It is only when human beings live within their limitations as creatures that they can find fulfilment. The desire to overstep limits can come from the individual in search of knowledge (3:5), or from the group in their striving for greatness and their drive for fame and recognition independently of God (11:4). The achievements of civilisation, good in themselves, mask the possibility of overstepping creaturely limits, and so God's intervention takes on the nature of a preventative character. God's intervention, resulting in the division of humanity into different peoples and languages, sets the scene for the beginning of history as we experience it. The story also sets the stage for the call of Abraham through whom the divisions introduced at Babel will ultimately be undone when 'all the families of the earth' are blessed (Gn 12:3). It sets in motion the history of salvation which is God's solution to the problem of Babel (Acts 2:1–11).

Conclusion

The opening chapters of Genesis are the result of new experiences and reflection on life on the part of a particular people, the Israelites, that signal an advance and a breakthrough to a new stage in human self-understanding in that they articulate something that is enduringly true about human beings and the world in which they live. Genesis 1–11 in its final form is a late component of the Bible. The stories now function as a backdrop to the history of the Old Testament people.

Genesis 1–11 gives a concrete synthesis of the Israelite view of God, human beings, the world and society. It witnesses to a progression within Israel's national consciousness towards universalisation. This, in time, was facilitated by the prophets and came to maturity during the experience of the Exile. Sometime after the Exile, the traditions were fused into the grand synthesis we find in Genesis 1–11. Conscious of the history and destiny of their people, gifted individuals within the community gradually became aware of the most profound problems of human existence which opened out to embrace all humankind – consciousness of limits, finitude, culpability, guilt, suffering, etc. They succeeded in articulating a universal consciousness, of which Genesis 1–11 is the literary expression.

The authors appropriated language and symbols of the surrounding cultures to articulate their own original vision of the world and humankind through patterns of thought which facilitated concrete expression of the universal in narrative form as distinct from philosophical or theological discourse. In putting forward their explanation of the human condition, they tried to account for the presence of evil, suffering and death. These realities were regarded as consequent on options chosen by human beings themselves. The individual stories describe the various ways in which human beings introduce evil into God's good world.

The stories contained in Genesis 1–11 are paradigmatic or typical. They are historical in the sense that they portray fundamental experiences common to all human beings from the dawn of history to the present and for all time. History begins with the human race and encompasses the constants and the variables which accompany the history of all peoples. Humans are and remain such as they have been described – creatures, limited, yet restless and inclined to overstep limits in their bid for total autonomy and mastery of life, but unable to achieve them by their own efforts alone and so continually frustrated. Humanity exists in time and space with all its potentialities and limitations. Created as personal beings by God, capable of entering into a relationship with him and with each other in community life, they are called to provide for their basic needs by work that makes cultural achievements possible. In their desire to transcend their present situation, however, they attempt to overstep limits that brings only suffering and frustration. They need God to curb them so that they can remain human.

The stories arose out of a sense of wonder and questioning, experiences of limits, suffering and guilt as well as events in the history of the Israelite people. These in turn gave rise to reflection on the fundamental problems of existence which expanded to embrace all humankind. They articulated the insights they gained in the form of stories that account for the presence of evil in the world. The evil experienced is twofold: evil submitted to as part of sinful creaturely existence – the tension between the sexes, pain in childbearing, hardship in work, fatigue and death; and evil committed, or moral evil, that has to do with freedom and choice – the transgressions of the first couple, Cain's murder of Abel, the revenge of Lamech, polygamy, widespread corruption, impiety, hubris and the desire for fame.

Nevertheless, despite its flaws, creation, including humankind, is good because it comes from the hands of a good Creator. Created for life, humans are set on a journey towards the tree of life (immortality), but if they are to reach that goal, they must live within the boundaries proper to created beings. Since they have freedom of choice, however, they may decide to take another path by choosing, not in accordance with the order of creation, but with what they themselves determine. This alternative can never satisfy their inbuilt yearning for fulness of life and love. Human beings by themselves cannot achieve total happiness, which is why Genesis 1–11 ends on an unfinished note. It is *God* who intervenes in the call of Abraham (Gn 12:1ff.) to set in motion his plan for the happiness of all people, reaching its climax in Jesus Christ who came 'that they may have life and have it in abundance' (Jn 10:10).

Genesis 1–11 provides realistic answers in story form to existential questions that arise from the experience of living in the world. Human beings live in God's world, a good world, a fitting habitat to prepare people to arrive at their final destination to be with God for all eternity. However, humans have difficulty in maintaining a balance in those relationships that would ensure harmony, happiness and joy in living their lives. Fractured relationships, the result of the misuse of freedom, cause hurt, suffering, evil and corruption when they disobey God's word. It seems that human beings are unable by themselves to sustain those relationships that make for happiness and fulfilment. What will happen now? Will God cast them off forever? In its rapport with God, Israel found answers to the fundamental problems of existence marked by evil, suffering and death, but also enveloped by the care and concern of a loving God.

The most striking characteristics of the God in these chapters are not his majesty and transcendence, but his compassion and concern for humanity as a whole. This is the God whom Israel later met in the course of its history. The Saviour of Israel is also the Creator of the world and humankind. God preserves the whole and stands in relationship with those nations outside the people of God throughout the whole course of human history. He created the world and keeps it in existence through his providence. The end of history and the world, like the beginning, is in God's hands. In the in-between, God calls Abraham, forms a people and guides them through history, culminating in the coming and mission of Jesus Christ which now continues in his Church till the end of time.

***

To gain some insights on how we can open ourselves to God's initiative, we will now retrace the principal stages of the journey of the spiritual evolution which Israel experienced, affirmed and deepened during the course of several centuries. That journey begins with the experience of Abraham. In the form in which they have come down to us, the patriarchal narratives begin with the genealogy of Abraham's ancestors (Gn 11:27–32) and end with the sons of Jacob in Egypt (Gn 50). These narratives witness to the existence of the patriarchs (c.1850–1700 BC) and to their spiritual experiences which were elaborated in the course of transmission to illuminate the truth of the original experiences.

Through Moses, the Israelite people acquired a community expression of the patriarchal religious experience. The pre-exilic prophets deepened and helped interiorise that experience. The reflections of the post-exilic wisdom teachers pondered the role that God the Creator through his providence plays in everyday life as a guide to individual successful living. In the centuries before the coming of Christ, the faithful remnant in Judaism lived and transmitted a profound religious experience that found expression in the prayers of the Psalter. We will select representative passages in the Old Testament that will facilitate our pursuit of the spiritual journey of the Israelite people to aid us in our anthropological study.

Endnotes

1   Bruce Vawter, *On Genesis: A New Reading,* London: G. Chapman, 1977, p. 97.

2   Here I am drawing on Benedict XVI, *Deus Caritas Est* (*God is Love*), London: Catholic Truth Society, nos. 2–11.

3   Nahum M. Sarna, *Understanding Genesis,* New York: Schocken Books, 1970, p. 53.

CHAPTER FOUR:
PATRIARCHS – NEW ORDER OF THE SOUL

The Call of Abraham[1]

The Abraham cycle which begins with Genesis 12:1–4 serves as an entrance into the story of the patriarchs. It was shaped in such a way as to link the patriarchal narratives to the primeval story, 'all the families of the earth' (11:9), and at the same time pointed beyond this to the history of the people of Israel, 'into a great nation'. God commands and Abram (later called Abraham) carries out the command. God's introductory address is divided into a command and a promise that is linked with it. There is also progression: the promise of blessing is made to an individual called Abraham, goes beyond him to those with whom he comes into contact, and eventually affects the whole of humanity. The phrase 'to bless' occurs five times and so sets the tone. Blessing becomes the catchword of Israel's history. It brings about greatness and renown, security and protection. God's action is not limited to Abraham and his posterity but reaches its goal only when it includes all the families of the earth. God's command finds a ready response in the soul of Abraham.

We are dealing here with a new point of departure in the history of humanity. One man is addressed by God in the midst of a multitude of nations. God is the subject of the first verb and thus is the subject of the entire subsequent history. The address begins with a command for Abraham to abandon all natural roots – land, clan, family – and to entrust himself to God's guidance. From a multitude of nations, God chooses a man, Abraham, and makes him the beginning of a new people and the recipient of great promises of blessing for all the nations. Genesis 1–11 finds its conclusion and indeed its *key* in this text. This is the significance of the universal preface to the peculiar history of Israel – human beings left to themselves are incapable of saving themselves, they need a saviour.

To the external geographical journey of Abraham there corresponds an interior spiritual journey of searching for religious truth and openness to it. It was to such an open soul that God revealed himself progressively, first in Ur (Gn 15:7) and later in Haran (Gn 12:1). Abraham follows that journey which corresponds interiorly to his encounter with God to whom he opens himself more and more. The abruptness of the opening verse (12:1) leaves the impression of something unusual in such a departure and underlies its religious character. What prompted Abraham to take such a drastic step was his prior searching for meaning in life that launched him on a demanding journey of faith and fidelity, punctuated by encounters with God along the way.

Genesis 15 stands at the heart of the Abraham cycle of stories (chs. 12–25). God makes promises to Abraham and his response in *faith* is emphasised. This was later elaborated (ch. 17), passed on and acquired significance for later generations – the promise of a son is combined with the promise of many descendants; the simple promise of land is combined with an oath. The promise of offspring is met by Abraham's believing faith: 'Abram put his faith in the Lord, who counted this as making him justified' (15:6).

Anthropological Perspectives

From the primeval history, human beings emerge as creatures in the likeness of God, superior to all other creatures because they are endowed with knowledge and freedom. But they have difficulty finding the right balance in existence and attempt to become like God by throwing off the limitations of creatureliness. They are then thrust back to an understanding of their condition by God and are made aware of the precariousness of their existence. They are taught that there is no one world of humanity rivalling heaven, but only the humble adjusting of society to the cosmic order made so by the Creator.

We are now presented with an obscure individual, Abraham, called by God to leave his homeland and settle in a foreign country to found a community through whom all the nations of the earth will be blessed. The spiritual fall from being which is the essence of sinfulness has now regained its equilibrium in the person of Abraham who has opened his soul to the word of God in faith and trust. A new order, a new balance is established in the soul of Abraham; his is the life of a person who puts his trust in God alone. So then, from the descendants of those dispersed after the abortive enterprise of Babel, God singles out one man who opens his soul to God's influence and who, in turn, opens up a new horizon before him. The pilgrimage of Abraham begins a new kind of history, although as yet it is a reality only in the soul of Abraham. In contrast to the ambitious builders of the tower of Babel who aspired to make a name for themselves, it is *God* who will make Abraham great. Accordingly, Israel's greatness will not lie in ambitious achievements measured by worldly standards, but in God who is active in its history to overcome the disharmony, violence and confusion sketched in the primeval history.

Abraham was open and ready to hear God's call, some kind of mystical experience perhaps, a direct eruption of the divine in his life which pointed a way for him. He must have had a sensitivity and openness to God which enlarged his perception beyond the normal range. The experience of Abraham is not transmitted in concepts but is expressed in the visual language typical of storytellers. We must get behind the mode of expression to the original historical experience, one that was spiritual, interior, an opening of the soul to the transcendent God which in turn modified and changed the whole external course of Abraham's life and behaviour.

It seems then that Abraham became dissatisfied with the ancestral gods of Mesopotamia and this crisis precipitated a personal search that set him on the road to discovering the true God. One day he became conscious of being in relationship with this God, the result of a gratuitous divine intervention in his life. Presupposed is a process of gradual openness on the part of Abraham to God, for there is no hint that God imposed himself on Abraham or forced his hand in any way. The experience is expressed in the language of relationships. Abraham experienced himself in relationship with God who is revealed as living, personal and beckoning. Abraham has found what he has been searching for, the answer to his quest, a spiritual enlightenment, an *illumination* which will enable him to set out on a long, difficult and exacting journey. If we deny this experience on the part of Abraham, then we are faced with the inexplicable phenomenon of a fidelity which rested on nothing in the lives of those who lived it. This runs counter to the contemporary milieu and to what we know about human nature.

The experience of Abraham can be summed up in three elements: the reality of God to whom he progressively opens himself, the interior acceptance of journeying which the invitation of God called forth, namely, the experience of faith, and the hope of life for the future which resulted from it. Later traditions highlight the essential truth of Abraham's experience. The reality of God is clearly distinguished from all other gods of the surrounding cultures and became known as the 'God of our fathers' until the time of Moses.

The generous response of Abraham in fidelity, trust and hope is evident in the spiritual journey of Abraham to the point of being willing to give up his whole hope for the future in the sacrifice of his beloved son of the promise, Isaac (Gn 22:1–19). We are alerted in verse one that this is a test of obedience. It allows us to appreciate the depths of commitment on the part of Abraham to his God which alone gives an adequate explanation of it. Abraham passed the test, and the promises are reiterated (vv. 16–18), articulating the content of the relationship between God and Abraham. They are formulated in the language of blessing, posterity which embraces the future, and possession of land which gives security. These direct attention to the only way to life – they point to the God of life that in turn evokes faith, trust and hope.

Biblical faith begins with Abraham who was someone who knew that God was speaking to him and who shaped his life on that basis. This God is not one of a particular nation, but of a particular person, Abraham. His power is not restricted by geography, country or people. This personal God accompanied Abraham to guard and guide him wherever he goes. Nor is this God restricted by the limitations of time – his speaking bears on the future as a promise of blessings of land and progeny. For Abraham, this meant an attitude of looking beyond the present moment, reaching out for something greater. The story of Abraham, therefore, can be viewed as the story of a struggle in overcoming obstacles in order to have faith and trust in God. This God has something to do with human dignity; he shows his care on the one hand, and rejection of what may damage that dignity on the other, as the judgment of Sodom and Gomorrah shows (Gn 18:16–19:29). The Israelite tradition ascribes this destruction to the moral depravity of these cities.

In this call and this road which was taken, Israel saw not only an event in her earliest history, but also a basic characteristic of her whole existence before God. Taken from the community of nations (cf. Num 23:9) and never truly rooted in Canaan, but even there a stranger (cf. Lev 25:23; Ps 39:12), Israel saw herself being led on a special road whose plan and goal lay completely in Yahweh's hand.[2]

The author of the epistle to the Hebrews succinctly sums up the experience of Abraham:

> By faith Abraham obeyed when he was called to set out for a place that he was to receive as an inheritance; and he set out, not knowing where he was going. By faith he stayed for a time in the land he had been promised, as in a foreign land, living in tents, as did Isaac and Jacob, who were heirs with him of the same promise. For he looked forward to the city that has foundations, whose architect and builder is God. (Heb 11:8–10)

This experience of God did not die with Abraham. The patriarchal narratives trace a line through Isaac and Jacob to the twelve tribes of Israel, the story of Joseph, and their sojourn in Egypt (chs. 25–50). In the intervening history, between the patriarchs and the time of Moses, a trickle of that experience must have continued, strong enough to broaden out into the constitution of Israel in the Mosaic covenant.

Endnotes

1   For an extended exposition on this subject, see Claus Westermann, *Genesis 12–36*, London: SPCK, 1986.

2   Gerhard von Rad, *Genesis: A Commentary*, London: SCM Press, 1963, p. 154.

CHAPTER FIVE:
MOSES AND THE PEOPLE OF GOD

Exodus

The Book of Exodus tells the story of the slavery of the Israelites in Egypt, the call of Moses, the escape from slavery, the Sinai experience of covenant with its stipulations (Decalogue), and the building of the Tabernacle as the locus of worship. The dramatic story begins with the oppression of the Israelites in Egypt, the birth, upbringing and call of Moses who is obliged to flee to Midian to escape the wrath of Pharaoh. In the silence of the desert, Moses is able to hear the voice of God commissioning him to lead God's people out of slavery. The revelation of the God of the fathers to Moses (Ex 3:1–4:17) is organised in a series of scenes. While tending the flocks of his father-in-law, Moses arrives at Horeb, the mountain of God. God appears to him in a flame of fire in the midst of a bush. Although it burns, the bush is not consumed, and Moses goes to look at this strange sight. The divine presence has captured his attention. God identifies himself as the God of the fathers and, when Moses has assumed a proper attitude of receptivity, God sends him to lead 'his people' out of slavery.

The burning bush episode (Ex 3:1–15) should be read with imagination and empathy – the curiosity of Moses, the divine presence, the calling of Moses by name, the giving of a new mission to lead the people to freedom, the revelation of the divine name. Moses manifests repeated misgivings concerning his ability to rescue his people until God assures him that he will be with him. The name, 'I am who I am' *('ehyeh 'asher 'ehyeh*, v. 14), emphasises the mystery of God – God simply is, and is a God who is present to help. A name also implies the ability to speak, to hear, to answer, it denotes God's personal nature. The God of Israel is living and personal, not a local God, but a God of the people and so not bound to any one place, a God who is near at hand to rescue his people from servitude. This God is also the God of the patriarchs. Moses becomes conscious of a personal presence that is hidden and transcendent, wholly other, yet near as one who can be called upon and responds. The God of Israel is inaccessible, yet accessible, transcendent yet near at hand. The God of Abraham and the fathers becomes the God of Israel, a God who is active in history, gives hope and security, and promises freedom in contrast to the pagan gods who are lifeless and oppressive. Such a revelation had to be dramatically shaped and presented in attractive colours for the purpose of narrative, for momentous events in human history cannot be told in any other way. The exodus from Egypt was an historical event through which God became Israel's liberator. This is highlighted in the literary presentation of the exodus narrative.

Exodus 1–15 is a dramatic unity consisting of the following major scenes: the opposition to Jacob's descendent in Egypt; the infancy and early life of Moses, his call and commission; the contest with Pharaoh, the so-called 'plagues' culminating in the death of the firstborn and the Passover ritual; the flight from Egypt and the victory at the Red Sea; and a concluding hymn. An historical drama unfolds in Exodus 1–15.[1] The protagonist is the God of Israel who intervenes on behalf of Israelite slaves. The plot of the drama is God's contest with Pharaoh, the divine representative of the Egyptian empire. The plot is developed in a series of suspense-filled episodes (the ten plagues). The ending comes when the Egyptian pursuers are drowned in the waters of the Red Sea and the Israelites escape to freedom. The theme of the drama is the action and triumph of the God of Israel that comes to the fore in the drama of the plagues. As the plagues follow one another, they gradually reveal the superiority of the God of Israel which is pointed up in the narrative. In all of this, Moses plays an essential, though subordinate, role.

The community of Israel retold and relived this exodus drama at its Passover celebrations. These historical experiences are therefore expressed in the language of worship, not journalistic prose, as the best medium to communicate the *meaning* of the historical event to the contemporary worshipping community who shared in and celebrated it. What is portrayed and highlighted in the exodus drama is a conflict of a *spiritual* order. As the plagues follow one another in the narrative, they reveal the superiority of the God of Israel. The conflict continues in a long, drawn-out battle until darkness envelops the land of Egypt (ninth plague), the first-born of the Egyptians are slain (tenth plague) and Pharaoh is reluctantly obliged to let the Israelites depart. The proper response only came with reluctance, hesitation and resistance, first on the part of Moses himself, then of Pharaoh and finally of the people. We are reminded how difficult and prolonged such a struggle can be. This is a confrontation between light and darkness, between good and evil, between the true God and the anti-God forces represented by Pharaoh: 'I will bring judgment on all the gods of Egypt, I am Yahweh' (12:12). The core of the historical events was then a clash between the God of Israel and the cosmological order of the Egyptian empire, a unique event in history. This new spiritual order had its origin in Moses' response to a divine revelation. God takes the initiative and speaks to Moses and Moses becomes conscious of God's presence as a personally beckoning encounter that has to do with his oppressed people. The paschal ceremony commemorated and re-lived this historical event which established the identity of the people of Israel on the basis of God's act of deliverance. It was both a sacrifice and a banquet.

Covenant

What began with the revelation from the burning bush was completed through the revelation from Sinai. The creation of the Israelite community through the covenant at Sinai is the second act in the drama by which the new dispensation was established. This is narrated in Exodus 19–24. The gift of revelation requires acceptance in order that it may become the form of historical existence. There is the preparation before God descends on Mount Sinai (19:1–25), and the covenant is sealed through a cultic act (24:3–11). Its ratification included the covenant stipulations ('words', *debarim*, vv. 3, 8) that refer to the Ten Words, commonly called the Ten

Commandments, or Decalogue. They are the articulation of the essentials of human community existence in the present under God.

The rescue from Egypt is inseparably related to the covenant at Sinai (Ex 19:3–6); the former is a preparation for the latter. The Exodus is oriented towards communion with God, a promise contingent on Israel's fidelity. The Israelites arrive at Sinai (Ex 19:1) and do not depart until Numbers 10:11. The remaining chapters of Exodus are concerned with the giving and ratification of the covenant and the erection of the tabernacle. The book of Leviticus continues the legislation given by God to Moses at Sinai. The laws (ritual of sacrifices, ceremony of ordination, laws regarding legal purity, the code of holiness) serve to teach the Israelites that they must always keep themselves in a state of external sanctity as a sign of their intimate union with the Lord. The central idea is: 'Be holy, because I, Yahweh your God, am holy' (Lev 19:2). The first ten chapters of Numbers are concerned with preparation for departure from Sinai.

God's descent on Mount Sinai is described in such a way as to evoke awe and reverence (Ex 19:16–25).[2] The content of the covenant relationship is summed up in the Decalogue (Ex 20:1–17) which is duly ratified in a sacred rite that contains a solemn promise of binding obligation (Ex 24:1–11). Once God and Israel have been solemnly joined together, the action turns towards establishing a permanent dwelling-place for God in the midst of his people (Ex 25ff.). Worship and covenant are inseparably interlocked. The covenant cannot be properly observed unless worship is at its heart.

The departure from Egypt was then the starting point for a communal experience of new life under God, a new way of living as a fitting response to the God who revealed himself. But this response only came with reluctance, for it is not easy to break with the past. The creation of the Israelite community through a covenant relationship brought with it a new order of living whereby Israel became God's special people, priestly representatives of the nations, a holy nation set apart that would bring blessings on the whole world (Ex 19:5–7).

Covenant is a sacred family bond uniting the parties in a permanent way, solemnised and enforced by oaths. As a symbol, it served to articulate a new kind of reciprocal, though unequal, *relationship* between God and the people of Israel. Moses mediates the covenant at Sinai complete with oaths, sacrificial ritual, familial meal and laws (ch. 24). The Sinai covenant with its attendant laws is oriented towards forming Israel into a holy people able to commune with God through worship. Genesis sees the world as a place of worship (Gn 2:3), and Exodus tells the story of the creation of Israel as a worshipping people.

The covenant law is summed up in the Decalogue, addressed to 'you' in the singular. It contains eight prohibitions and two positive commandments to stake out limits and freedom of action within these limits. New behaviour, new conduct is necessary to become a new people in response to revelation. The Decalogue facilitated the journey towards true life and freedom and became the social expression of the covenant relationship. Its ratification took place by means of a sacred rite including an altar, sacrifice, reading of the law and response by the people: 'We will observe all the commands that the Lord has decreed' (24:3). The sprinkling of blood (the seat of life) on the altar (representing God) and on the people forged a new, indissoluble bond (24:5-6). The Decalogue became the new charter, a new constitution, the contents of which were to be internalised and lived out in daily life. The first three commandments forbid what would obscure the presence of the transcendent God. The worship of other gods would compromise the uniqueness of the God of Israel, while images can be used to control and manipulate God. The last five commandments serve to protect the basic goods of life, marriage, property, social honour and covetousness (envy). Two positive commandments protect right relations with God through time by keeping the Sabbath holy, and the honouring of parents assures harmony between the generations.

> The Decalogue was the charter of freedom which Yahweh had presented to his people delivered from Egypt. The people received it not as a burden, but as a gift which was seen as a privilege and as an occasion for thanks.[3]

The Decalogue contains the essential ingredients for human existence in community in the present under God. The first three deal with the relationship between God and Israel; the other seven govern the relationship among fellow Israelites. The Decalogue spells out exactly what it means to be holy in relation to God and fellow humans. What is known as the Covenant Code (Ex 20:22–23:33) contains more specific applications of the Decalogue and includes civil and penal laws, regulation of ritual, and social morality suited to a settled way of life in an agricultural community. The right order of living will be assured in a community attuned to the hidden God when it is not disturbed by the anti-divine rebellion of pride or the anti-human rebellion of envy which enclose the Decalogue. These essentials will be made more specific in the legal tradition which was developed and applied in the community at different periods of its existence (Ex 21–23; Lev 17–26; Deut 12–26).

> In the Old Testament tradition, the decisive action of Moses' activity as mediator is not the act of leading the people out of Egypt but the act of handing on the Law at Mount Sinai. It is only through this that the exodus from the foreign land takes on meaning and stability. For the people is set free and becomes a free nation of its own only by becoming a legal community ... a Law that is truly justice, namely, right order in relation to one another, in relation to Creation and in relationship to the Creator.[4]

True justice and, with it, freedom can come into existence only when the true God is properly recognised, when humans become properly aware of who they are and order their existence in a life with others on the basis of God's law. The goal of the Exodus was the securing of a place to worship God in the way willed by him and so it is from Sinai, where the covenant with God was forged, and from which Israel's law proceeds. This law ensures justice and so builds up a right relationship with God, with others and with all creation. But these relationships which guarantee freedom depend on the covenant – the fundamental relationship that orders all others, namely, the relationship with God. The goal of the Exodus then was to make Israel into a people with its own freedom and dignity as it carried out its own historical mission.

Living the Covenant Relationship

The meaning of the Decalogue is determined both by context and content. With the conclusion of the covenant, it becomes the *constitution* for a new people, addressed to Israel collectively and to each individually. Its content is not merely rules but the ingredients of a new divine *order*, a new way of living in the world that becomes effective and life-changing only when its contents are internalised. That is why the central movement of the Pentateuch is to and from Sinai with Leviticus forming its centrepiece. This suggests that the goal of the Mosaic instruction is communion with God and his people through the liturgy in a liturgically shaped lifestyle.

Moses had to communicate an awareness of God's presence to the people because it demanded a response. He had to facilitate the living out of that relationship. Covenant relationships in ancient cultures were also social contracts based on liturgy and law. And so the law comprising the Decalogue and the legal tradition embraced the religious, moral, social, economic and political spheres of living. It spelt out what was involved in respect for life in its vertical and horizontal dimensions for the journey to freedom and happiness. The law was meant to foster a living relationship when its contents were interiorised rather than merely observed.

The celebration of liturgical rites strengthened that bond and gave rise to the liturgical traditions associated with the Temple (Leviticus). The rites and sacrifices served as a means of renewal, purification and internalisation. God's saving interventions were recalled and celebrated during the great feasts and covenant renewal ceremonies. Law and liturgy then served as a means of deepening relationships when the contents were internalised and lived out on a daily basis. However, these means were in no way automatic, or a form of magic. The observance of the law could degenerate into legalism; the liturgy could become mere external routine. The prophets' task would be to facilitate passing beyond legalism and external observance to a personal encounter with the God of life and love.

The Promised Land is the space for worship and sacrificial liturgy, which in turn became the means by which the covenant relationship with God is renewed and maintained, and communion with God is actualised and experienced. The Book of Leviticus, at the heart of the Pentateuch, spells out concepts of sacrifice, priesthood and laws of cleanliness and holiness. Communion with God takes place through the liturgy and a unique lifestyle that is necessary to foster and maintain that communion.

Israel received the gift of the land to fulfil the promise to Abraham so that worship of the true God could take place there. And so, something more than mere possession was involved. It fulfilled the promise to Abraham only when it became a place where God abides and reigns (Ex 15:17–18), that is, where God's will is carried out and a proper existence befitting God's people is lived out on a daily basis. It is only when the relationship with God is rightly ordered that all other relationships – with others, with creation – will be in order. Consequently, what took place at Sinai gave meaning to the possession of the land where the people were free to live the truth of their humanity.

> What emerged from the alembic of the desert was not a people like the Egyptians or Babylonians, the Canaanites or Philistines, the Hittites or Arameans, but a new genus of society, set off from all civilisations of the age by divine choice. It was a people that moved on the historical scene while living towards a goal beyond history.[5]

Endnotes

1   Bernhard W. Anderson, Steven Bishop and Judith H. Newman, 'Liberation from Bondage', in *Understanding the Old Testament* (5th edn), New Jersey: Prentice Hall, 2007, pp. 48–75.

2   Anderson *et al.*, 'Covenant in the Wilderness', *op. cit.*, pp. 76–100.

3   Eric Voegelin, *Order and History, vol. 1: Israel and Revelation (The Collected Works of Eric Voegelin, vol. 14)*, (M. Hogan, ed.), Columbia: University of Missouri Press, 2001, pp. 466–480. See also, Johann J. Stamm and Maurice E. Andrew, *The Ten Commandments in Recent Research*, London: SCM Press, 1967, p. 114.

4   Jospeh Ratzinger, *A Turning Point for Europe,* San Francisco: Ignatius Press, 1994, p. 73.

5   Voegelin, *Israel and Revelation*, p. 154.

CHAPTER SIX:
BIBLICAL HISTORIOGRAPHY

Introduction¹

Biblical writers produced an extensive historical narrative that ranges from the conquest of the Promised Land to the fall of Jerusalem. It is a unique symbolism that grew to its final form through centuries of historiographic work as well as absorbing oral traditions that went further back. This work contains stories as symbolisations of experiences with genuine history intertwined. There are then two foci to the presentation of Israelite history: the creation of a community through Moses and the covenant, and the creation of a political organisation for successful pragmatic existence under the monarchy. These will later on be differentiated into sacred and profane history, into Church and State.

Soon after the establishment of the monarchy in Israel it became obvious that the new social order did not correspond to the intentions of the covenant. We see the interplay of experiences in the struggle of the spirit for freedom from its confinement within a particular social organisation in the land of Canaan. It was this struggle that determined the unique structure of the biblical narrative as a literary work that became paradigmatic world history. The people of Israel had to contend with two experiential forces that, on the one hand, pushed towards full realisation of life under God and, on the other, pulled the people towards mundane existence and away from God. These two counteracting forces met in the creation of this historiographic work. Pragmatic events then acquired a symbolic meaning as fulfilment of, or defections from, the covenant order of life, or as compromises between the will of God and the conditions of worldly existence. Later historians would heighten events paradigmatically in the light of the covenant order, but they did not destroy a history that itself had become a symbol of revelation. History as the present under God became the inner form of Israelite existence.

The books of Joshua, Judges, 1–2 Samuel and 1–2 Kings tell the story of Israel's possession and sojourn in the Promised Land till the time of the Exile. It begins with Joshua and the twelve tribes taking control of the land. The story continues with accounts of 'judges' (charismatic figures) who led Israel in securing its presence in the land. This was followed by narratives of Israelite kings, the loss of the land and Israel in exile. The rabbis called these books 'the Former Prophets' because they associated them with prophetic authorship. Scholars refer to them as 'the Deuteronomic History of Israel' because the book of Deuteronomy provided the theological principles that guided the telling of that story. These books, however, are not history in the modern sense of the term. Their homiletic character is evident from beginning to end. The books as we have them date from the time of the Exile or shortly after, and so the story of Israel in the Promised Land turns Israel's past into an extended sermon to provide the exiles with some basis for hope in the future.

Ancient biblical history was less concerned with reporting in detail the facts of the situation than with explaining the meaning of those facts. Its primary purpose was to disclose the action of the living God in the affairs of human beings. It is called 'sacred history' because it highlights the divine or supernatural dimension of that history. In this way, Israel's past held the key to the future. The books stress the importance of serving the Lord alone by shaping one's conduct according to the norms of Israelite morality as found in the Deuteronomic Code (Deut 12–26). They reveal what happens when Israel is obedient and when Israel is disobedient. The narratives assert that Israel can have a future because God has set before it the choice of life or death (Deut 30:15–20). If Israel chooses the path of obedience, it can have a future in the land. The immediate purpose of this history, therefore, was to stimulate faith and hope in the exiles living in Babylon by reminding them that Israel came to possess the land because of God's power and leadership. It was able to receive the land as God's gift through its obedience because it was *God* who made it possible for them to take control of their lives and destinies.

The story of Israel as told in these books was an answer to the questions of the exiles: Has God utterly rejected us and, if so, why? Consequently, the story is best understood as a response to questions such as these. It was written to inculcate a spirit of obedience and commitment to the law of Moses if Israel were to have a future. That is why the books of Joshua and Judges, for example, are not simply the preservation of memories of the conquest and of charismatic leaders. They serve to illustrate the consequences of both obedience and disobedience to the Lord as the life of the tribes slowly degenerated into anarchy. The story of the establishment of the monarchy (1–2 Sm) is one of social innovation for the sake of survival. But it also shows what can happen, for example, when David is unable to keep in check the tendency to absolutise the institution of the monarchy and ignore fundamental moral values in his affair with Bathsheba (2 Sm 11–12).

The books of Kings reflect a clear bias in favour of Judah for none of the kings of Israel receives a positive evaluation. A few kings in Judah are praised, but most are condemned for promoting or at least allowing worship that compromised the uniqueness of the God of Israel. In this way, 1–2 Kings helped the exiles make sense of events that challenged their religious beliefs. They put in sharp focus the consequences of failing to remain absolutely committed to the Lord and to a pattern of life that ensured it. For election as the chosen people of God by itself offered no guarantee of survival. That is why what began with so much hope ended in disaster through self-destruction. But God's mercy triumphs over his justice and a renewed Israel emerged from the Exile.

Content[2]

The people of Israel spent forty years wandering in the desert before reaching the promised land. It was a time of grumblings, regrets, defections and revolts as well as renewals. There was tension between their frustrations occasioned by the hardships of the desert and their duty to show gratitude to God for their freedom. The episodes (Ex 15:22–18:27; Ex 32–34; Num 11–25) show the fragility of the people's loyalty despite the care and concern shown to them by God. There was need for constant purification if Israel were to succeed in possessing the land.

The Book of Joshua recounts the career of Joshua who led Israel into the land of Canaan, defeated enemies, divided the land among the twelve tribes and renewed the covenant (ch. 24) as a means of keeping the land. The account is stylised and employs hyperbole. The conquest is presented as a cultic act led by priests in a liturgical procession (chs. 3–4). The promised land was to become a place of worship of the true God. The Book of Judges recounts the history of Israel from the time of Joshua to the prophet Samuel. It was a time marked by religious, moral, social and political chaos that was alleviated by charismatic figures known as judges who delivered Israel from its enemies. Worship of the Lord was abandoned in favour of Canaanite idolatry. The story is told in repeated cycles of disobedience, punishment, repentance and restoration. We are given to understand the rationale for the institution of the monarchy with certain misgivings because of invasions by external enemies – in particular, the Philistines. The kingship was established by Saul and reached its high point under David.

In 1–2, Samuel, David is the central figure, and his life is recounted in detail. He marks the final transition from the rule of judges to hereditary kingship. The reason for his prominence lies in his reception of an everlasting covenant from God through the prophet Nathan (2 Sm 7:4–17) that in time became the focus of the eschatological hopes in Israel. David's sin with Bathsheba (2 Sm 11), however, marks the beginning of a decline. The books of Kings detail the history of David's successors, the divided monarchy and the collapse of his kingdom (960–587 BC). They include the glorious reign of Solomon with its climax in the building and dedication of the Temple (1 Kgs 8) after which there is a steady decline both spiritually and materially, culminating in the destruction of both the Temple and Jerusalem and the exile of the last remaining king. Despite the ministry of God's prophets, the royal sponsorship of illegitimate worship led first to the division and ultimately to the destruction of the kingdom of David.

A Unique Symbolism[3]

With Israel, a new type of history emerges that is primarily an account of Israel's relationship with its God as experienced by people who struggled for attunement with the transcendent God, yet with a pragmatic core. The course of events became sacred history; single events became paradigms or models of God's ways with human beings. Consequently, an event experienced in relation to God will be truthfully related if its essence as paradigm is carefully elaborated. Pragmatic details become less significant. What is important is the revealed will of God and the human response in obedience or disobedience. Original accounts were reworked to point up their paradigmatic essence by means of dramatisation until they were eventually integrated into a body of history with its own peculiar meaning that we find in the historical books of the Old Testament.

The united kingdom of David and Solomon was initially regarded as the climax of the Exodus and conquest, but ended in the divided kingdoms of Israel and Judah. The former disappeared in 721 BC, the latter in 587 BC when the people of God were exiled to Babylon. Yet 'something' remained. The Sinai covenant concerned only the divine–human relationship and the relations of fellow Israelites with each other. Israel had to borrow from its neighbours political and social institutions like kingship that enabled it to exist and organise itself for life in the world. A conflict ensued between the demands of the Sinai covenant, on the one hand, and the institution of kingship on the other, and this led to the decomposition of the Israelite order that is highlighted in the David–Bathsheba incident (2 Sam 11–12)[4] and subsequently to moral decay. It seems that mundane success threatened the distinctiveness of the Israelite people, but religious faith survived due in no small measure to the prophetic movement.

Israel also gave rise to a new type of political society with the transcendent God as the source of order, and so became the carrier of a new truth in history. The Old Testament record tells of the events surrounding the discovery of this truth and the course of Israelite history as the confirmation of that truth. Society exists under God and the history of Israel illustrates the striving for order within the world while attuning itself to the order of being beyond the world. It seems that the intention of the authors was to create a world history going back to creation (Gn 1–11) with Israelite history as the representative history of humanity when the historiographic work was appended to the Pentateuch.

Following the conquest of the land, Israelite history becomes the story of obedience and disobedience to the revealed will of God during the monarchy when king and people for the most part repudiated their heritage.[5] The carriers of meaning, then, became the prophets. In the post-exilic period the Old Testament was divided into *Torah* (or Pentateuch), *Prophets* and *Writings*. The *Torah* covered the period from the creation of the world and humanity to the constitution of Israel under the covenant. The *Prophets* were divided into the Former Prophets that traced the history of the conquest, confederacy and kingship but subordinated its interpretation to the preaching of the prophets, and the Latter Prophets, or the writing prophets (Isaiah, Jeremiah, Ezekiel and the twelve Minor Prophets). The *Writings* embraced the post-exilic literature (1, 2 Chronicles, Ezra-Nehemiah, Wisdom, Psalms and Apocalyptic literature). The chosen people gradually came to realise that community under God was not tied to Palestine. What finally emerged was a community that preserved its past as an eternal present for future generations. It still had a long way to go to re-join humankind from which it had separated so that the promise to Abraham could be fulfilled: 'All the tribes of the earth shall bless themselves by you' (Gn 12:3). Only with the emergence of Christianity as a worldwide movement did the sacred line re-join humankind.

The Old Testament narrative is, therefore, a unique symbolism which reached its final form over the course of several centuries. The uppermost layer of the historiographic work portrays the Israelite order as a historical form of existence in the present under God. The events recorded were transformed into a drama where pragmatic history was subordinated to its deepest meaning. For example, Exodus 1–15 is not a report of events as such, but a cultic glorification of the God of Israel who in that historic event created his people. Events are now transformed into a drama portraying the victory of Israel's God over the anti-God forces represented by Pharaoh. Genesis through Kings, then, is not primarily pragmatic history in the modern sense, but paradigmatic world history with its nucleus in the time of Moses and the constitution of the people of the covenant.

It soon became evident, however, that the new social order of kingship did not correspond to the demands of the covenant. Israel had survived as a political community but had betrayed the Mosaic law. It was the task of the prophets to make clear that political success was no substitute for obedience to covenant law and that social advancement was no proof of righteousness before God. What is narrated, therefore, is the struggle for freedom from confinement within a particular social order and this determined the structure of the historiographic work. The Old Testament narrative became a new kind of symbolism that brought about a new form of existence under God. Because the God who spoke and acted is transcendent, his words and deeds are valid for all time and become the key to unlocking the understanding of the presence, deed and command of God in every present moment.

The Old Testament historical books, then, offer a theology of history. Events and personalities have a typical and symbolic value. Since human beings are endowed with free will, there will always be a conflict between obedience and disobedience to God's will – a perennial battle between good and evil. Conscious of this, the sacred writers drew lessons from Israel's past to illustrate this struggle for their contemporaries. This was their homiletic intention. Since they were inspired by God, their writings became the word of God that is valid for all time. It reminds us that the kingdom of God is forever being inaugurated in the midst of opposition until the forces of evil are finally vanquished and the kingdom of God is definitively established. In the meantime, God leads his people to salvation through the events of history. Since God acts in history, a mere chronicle of events would not do justice to this fact. The theological significance had to be highlighted to offer a basis for faith and hope and, accordingly, historical elements play a subordinate role.

So rather than inquiring into what actually happened, we ask what the text wishes to affirm and teach us today. For example, the Abraham cycle describes the divine promises and Abraham's response in faith as the deepest kernel of these events that are still relevant for us today (Rm 4). The exodus narrative is not primarily an account of ancient events but attests that God is still saving his people, evoking faith and hope in the context of the Passover liturgy. The events related are *typical* events of the way God always acts throughout history and so becomes paradigmatic – the 'kinds of things' God did, is doing and will do in the future, as well as typical responses on the part of the people. God is working both in creation and in history to save his people, and so the theological and pastoral significance of these events are highlighted. 'All these things happened to them as a warning, and it was written down to be a lesson for us who are living at the end of the age' (1 Cor 10:11).

Law of Extermination and Violence[6]

Difficulties arise when we read of repeated cases of violence and cruelty seemingly commanded by God. Already in Genesis 6:5–12 wickedness, violence and corruption are widespread in human society that later took the form of idolatry. Sacred scripture, then, has also a prophetic function by inviting people to recognise evil in order to resist and avoid it. For example, the law of extermination (*herem*) of the Canaanite towns was carried out by Joshua and later by kings who fought invading enemies. These narratives were written centuries later and so we must consider the meaning the authors intended to convey. The law of extermination is not to be taken literally as we shall see (cf. Mt 5:29–30).

Success in conquering and ongoing possession of the land of Canaan depended on fidelity to the covenant law that preserved the distinctive Israelite way of life. This identity was always under threat throughout the history of the Old Testament period, not least by the danger of assimilation to the surrounding environment to become 'like the nations' by adopting their idolatrous lifestyle. The need to preserve Israel's special identity governed the narratives on war, for co-existence in Canaan threatened both the identity and the existence of Israel (Deut 7:1–6; 20:1–20). The command to exterminate the enemy is therefore both hyperbolic and idealised, not history in the usual sense, but expressing deeper realities. For example, the conquest of Jericho took place, not by military conquest, but by fidelity to the law, at the heart of which is worship of God. The capture of Jericho took place by means of a liturgical procession (Jos 6:1–21)! The point being made is that it is fidelity to the law that guarantees conquest and continued possession of the land because it preserves the identity of God's people. And so, an incident from the past is recounted to give a lesson for the present, namely, eliminate everything that might distract from fidelity to

God and his law so that the descendants of Abraham can become a blessing for the nations. Conflicts are also presented as a clash between powerful enemies and Israel, which in comparison was weak and defenceless. There is as well the triumph of the weak when God casts down the mighty and raises up the lowly. The enemies of Israel, too, were guilty of crimes, for example, child sacrifice, debased worship, social injustice (Am 1:3–2:3) and so the narratives show the execution of divine justice carried out by Israel against them because of evils committed (cf. Wis 12:3–16). There is reckoning to be had whenever any nation, including Israel, is guilty of injustice and wrongdoing. Joshua and the Israelite leaders are regarded as executing justice. The narratives then became parables of judgment that must be balanced against other passages that announce the compassion and forgiveness of God. For the latter are the goal of every historical action on the part of God as well as being models for just actions on the part of human beings. Israelite historiography, then, is neither a chronicle of events nor pure fiction. It must be understood in context through a canonical reading of the Bible in a faith context as the word of God. A fundamentalist reading is, accordingly, to be avoided. We must pay attention rather to the historical and literary context to discern what the narratives were intended to convey.

The psalms also contain what appear to be expressions of hatred and desire for vengeance that are seemingly at odds with the love of enemies enjoined by Christ. How can these passages become prayers? Firstly, the literary genre of lament militates against taking these phrases literally. The prayers of lamentation or petition are made by people who are being unjustly persecuted, so there is a passionate supplication to God for help (Ps 109). The genre uses exaggeration and exasperated expressions both in describing suffering (Ps 22), the depth of feeling (Ps 139:21-22) and request for help which is motivated by the emotional state of those who are in a dramatic life and death situation (Ps 3:7). The images are metaphors requesting God to put an end to malignant forces that will destroy life in the future (Ps 137:8–9). They are 'deliver us from evil' prayers that ask God to administer justice, not expressions of personal vengeance.

Although the enemies of the psalmist are real people, they are presented as faceless. The situations described are typical, the language is conventional and metaphorical so that it can be applied to similar situations of conflict. The enemy is not only threatening physical life, but, more importantly, the spiritual life of the psalmist. Indeed, hostile forces are not only flesh and blood; there are also demonic forces from which the psalmist wishes to be delivered: 'For all the gods of the peoples are demons' (Ps 96:5, LXX; cf. Eph 6:12). The harsh and hyperbolic language expresses the incompatibility between good and evil, God and Satan.

The life of worship influenced the presentation of historical events by motivating ethical conduct when God's mighty deeds were recalled and made present in the liturgy. The prophetic denunciation of the cult was never understood subsequently as a rejection of the cult itself. In fact, Israel could never have preserved its distinctive way of life without the protective framework of the cult that had the effect of guiding the moral conduct of their lives. The prophetic critique served as a normative criticism against persistent and recurring *abuses* of religion that threaten authentic faith in every generation, including our own. It serves to purify motives, not abolish the cult. The struggle to align prayer and worship with ethical conduct remains our struggle and so the prophetic critique has relevance for us as well.

Endnotes

1   Victor H. Matthews, *101 Questions and Answers on the Historical Books of the Bible*, New Jersey: Paulist Press, 2009. For further reading, consult the following notes for bibliographical material.

2   Bernhard W. Anderson, Steven Bishop and Judith H. Newman, 'The Promised Land', in *Understanding the Old Testament* (5th edn), New Jersey: Prentice Hall, 2007, pp. 101–139.

3   Anderson *et al.* 'The Formation of an All-Israel Epic', *op. cit.*, pp. 139–166.

4   Eric Voegelin, *Order and History, vol. 1: Israel and Revelation (The Collected Works of Eric Voegelin, vol. 14)*, (M. Hogan, ed.), Columbia: University of Missouri Press, 2001, pp. 303–330.

5   Anderson *et al.*, 'The Struggle Between Faith and Culture', 'The Throne of David', *op. cit.*, pp. 167–194, 196–227.

6   Pontifical Biblical Commission, *The Inspiration and Truth of Sacred Scripture*, London: Catholic Truth Society, 2014.

CHAPTER SEVEN:
PROPHETS – INTERIORISATION OF THE COVENANT RELATIONSHIP

Introduction

The great achievement of the prophets was to regain a presence under God that was on the point of being lost through the sinfulness of both kings and people by spelling out concretely what must be done to restore order. They communicated God's word for the present moment and summoned the people to renewal. They interpreted and applied the demands of the covenant and kept alive the spiritual traditions that were all but forgotten. The prophets felt called by God as his spokespersons – 'Thus says the Lord ...' – and recalled the past to evoke a new response of commitment in the present. Through their preaching, the Mosaic message was brought to life in the present with a new vitality.

The people had to be reminded that continued existence as God's people depended on their response to God's revelation as interpreted by the prophets. The latter had to face two problems simultaneously: defection to foreign gods (idolatry) that raised the question of whether Israel was still the people of God and outward ritual observance rather than acting out of inner conviction. The prophets' most challenging task, however, was to clarify the meaning of existence in historical form. Furthermore, the appearance of solitary prophets in opposition to the people could not but raise the problem of personal existence under God, independent of Israel's collective existence.

The Elijah cycle (1 Kgs 17–19, 21) is an independent unit of tradition that was later incorporated into the history of the monarchy. It is primarily concerned with mirroring the experienced history of Israel in its encounter with God in the political and cultural crisis of the time (*c*.850 BC).[1] The Israelite king Ahab had married the pagan queen Jezebel who tried to impose her pagan religion on Israel and liquidate every vestige of Israel's traditional faith. Elijah led the voice of protest to warn of the dangers and restore the Sinaitic order. One of the most vivid episodes in the history of prophecy was the contest on Mount Carmel between Elijah and the prophets of Baal (1 Kgs 18:20–40). Elijah challenged the ambivalence of the people and called for exclusive allegiance to the God of Israel. The vivid narrative serves as a paradigmatic warning against the dangers of insidious and seemingly excusable compromises that threaten true faith in every age. Elijah had come to the realisation that the new existence under God could be lost and the covenant order undone. The encounter proved to be a decisive intervention on the part of Elijah after which the people repented and returned to God.

Another episode (ch. 21) occurred when King Ahab wished to purchase the family property of Naboth, who refused on the grounds that the real owner was God and insisted that he was not free to sell his ancestral land. But at the instigation of the king's wife, Jezebel, Naboth was falsely accused of blasphemy and treason in a trumped-up charge and stoned to death, after which Ahab took possession of the vineyard. However, when Elijah confronted the king and pointed out that the crime merited impending divine judgment, Ahab repented. The incident introduces the social message of the later prophets. God had created a covenant community in which each person, irrespective of social status, stood equal before the law. When a member was taken advantage of by the powerful, God intervened to defend the weak and defenceless. Covenant faith as preached by Elijah protested against these evils and encouraged social reform. This is why he is portrayed as the great spiritual opponent of the forces of the age because he succeeded in restoring the true order of the covenant. Spiritual authority was already passing from king to prophet.

Literary Prophets[2]

From the eighth to the sixth century BC, a succession of prophets arose whose preaching is preserved in writings that bear their name. They struggled to keep the faith alive, railed against abuses and became spiritual leaders, the conscience of the people. From the great beginnings under Moses and David to a precipitous spiritual decline, the rise of the prophets in the middle of the eighth century BC is also related to the rise of political superpowers. It was the Assyrian rise to power during the latter half of the eighth century BC to which Amos, Hosea and Isaiah (chs.1–39) responded. The decline of Assyria and the rise of Babylon a century later set the stage for Jeremiah and Ezekiel. The advent of Persia in the second half of the sixth century BC marked the opening of yet another wave of prophetic activity beginning with Second Isaiah (chs. 40–55) when the Israelite faithful remnant, purified by the ordeal of the Exile, returned to its homeland determined to begin life all over again in the land that God had given to them.

In the midst of their people's spiritual decline and the rise of pagan superpowers which threatened Israel's very existence, the prophets warned of dangers ahead. More importantly, they interpreted *why* these catastrophes were about to occur. And then, as the disasters descended, they sought to awaken hope in a new and better future. For the most part, the prophets were isolated figures who, prompted by a voice within them, acted alone to challenge the entire people to put away false gods and behave justly in their dealings with their neighbours. They may be characterised as inspired interpreters of their historical situation who accurately read 'the signs of the times'. They took a long and hard look at what was *really* wrong with their world and what was needed to set it right. Their prophecies of destruction and restoration gave rise to the conviction that their God alone was Lord of the whole world whose providence ruled over all.

Amos

Amos preached in the northern kingdom towards the end of the prosperous reign of Jeroboam II (786–746 BC).[3] But this prosperity concealed the seeds of social decay, despite a magnificent display of liturgy that gave only a false sense of security for it had little influence on day-to-day living. The practice of religion had become an alibi for a lifestyle devoid of justice and concern for the poor. Amos was castigating the participants, not condemning the cult as such. Religious practice had become a drug to tranquilise conscience rather than seeking God and doing his will: 'Seek good and not evil, that you may live; and so the Lord, the God of hosts, will be with you' (5:14).

As a prophet of divine judgment, the sovereignty of God in nature and in history dominates his thought. God will use neighbouring nations to bring judgment on Israel's oppressive self-indulgence and false worship. In particular, a callously indifferent lifestyle among the elite in the cities was an important factor in the spiritual decline. This was evident from his biting portrait of indolent wives (4:1–3) and luxury-loving husbands (6:4–7), whose self-indulgent lifestyles led to social injustice against the poor. Amos called the people back to the high moral and religious demands of the covenant. Exploitation, injustice, corrupt leadership, upper-class indifference and unfaithfulness were rampant (2:6–16; 4:1–5; 6:1–7; 8:4–14). In response to hypocritical worship and oppression of the poor, the cultural elite will experience oppression and exile.

As well as listing the crimes of Israel's neighbours (1:3–2:3), Amos cites crimes of individual Israelites against each other in times of peace (2:6–12), despite prior privileges and opportunities. Poor people were being sold into debt-slavery for next to nothing. Others were being forced to sell their small ancestral estates under pressure from an upper-class elite who were taxing them to death. Worse still, cloaks taken in pledge from the desperately poor were being kept beyond nightfall when they were needed for essential warmth while sleeping. Sexual morality and respect for others had broken down. A nation divided against itself in such a manner, Amos prophesied, cannot survive because God will not permit it to survive. Disaster is coming that will 'crush' the elite who are perpetrating such crimes.

It seems that a religiously inspired optimism had gripped the elite, the result of recently acquired material prosperity. Because of this, they were convinced that God was 'with them' (5:14) and there was the expectation that he might soon act on a certain 'day', in the not-too-distant future, to bring them to a position of unprecedented prominence. But Amos declared that they should have known better; it was disaster, not triumph, that lay ahead (5:18–20). Their complacency and neglect of justice arose from worship practices that were hypocritical. Amos' abhorrence of these practices is obvious from his famous diatribe (5:21–26). Though the external forms of worship were scrupulously observed, they distracted people and lulled them into thinking that their relationship with God was intact while the most elementary principles of social justice were neglected: 'I hate and despise your feasts, and I take no delight in your solemn assemblies. Even though you offer me your burnt offerings and cereal offerings, I will not accept them … Take away from me the noise of your songs; to the melody of your harps I will not listen. But let justice roll down like waters, and righteousness like an ever-flowing stream' (vv. 21–24). Amos was not suggesting that ritual should be replaced by social action. Rather social behaviour must correspond to what happens at the shrines; justice is a precondition for acceptable worship.

That the people would listen to Amos and change their ways was far from certain (3:12; 5:2–3; 8:11–12; 9:8). His task was, therefore, to forewarn them of the catastrophe itself and explain why it was coming. People would later understand that this occurred because of God's justice and integrity, his compassion for those who suffer and were wrongfully oppressed. God could no longer overlook a people's offences (7:8–9). Other prophets would be called upon to envision a future beyond a disaster that was now looming. The book ends with the prospects of restoration and prosperity (9:11–15) which seems to be a later addition. For restoration, not catastrophe, would be the end result of the prophetic preaching.

Hosea

Like Amos, Hosea was not content to warn his contemporaries of impending disaster. He also interprets why it was about to occur. From the time of entry into Canaan, the native cult of Baal posed a temptation for Israel that led to idolatry and syncretism in Hosea's time (2:13). Hosea discerned that the root cause of the social and political turmoil lay in the extent to which Canaanite religious practices had infiltrated Israelite worship (10:1–2; 13:1–3). Israel had accommodated itself to the Canaanite religion (syncretism) which included cultic prostitution while still worshipping their God

(4:12–14). This resulted in moral blindness: 'There is no fidelity, no tenderness, no knowledge of God in the country, only perjury and lies, slaughter, theft, adultery and violence, murder after murder' (4:1–2). This blindness was a recipe for self-destruction: 'Their deeds do not allow them to return to their God, since a prostituting spirit possesses them, and they do not recognise the Lord' (5:4).

Violence was especially manifest in the bloody coups perpetrated by Israel's rulers (6:9; 7:1, 7). Although Canaanite influence and lawless kings played their part in the widespread decadence of Israel, the main responsibility rested on the shoulders of the priests (4:4–9) who 'have rejected knowledge … and forgotten the teaching of your God' and so 'my people perish for want of knowledge' (4:6). There was a spiritual decline because the priests neglected to teach the people the 'knowledge' of God which would have prevented decay (4:2). What was missing was any real understanding of the basic covenant stipulations that should have guided Israel's conduct. The degradation of the priestly office in particular was the ultimate tragedy of God's people (5:1–7).

Despite the widespread corruption, Hosea was hopeful for the future. This hope was derived from the nature of God (11:1–9). Notwithstanding the people's persistent disloyalty, the Lord cannot bring himself to annihilate his people. His love for Israel is so great that compassion triumphs over vengeance: 'Ephraim, how could I part with you? Israel, how could I give you up?' (v. 8). Judgment must come, but it will be a preparation for that day in which Israel will be restored and reunited with its God with the tenderness of a husband winning back the affections of his estranged wife (2:4–25). Hosea's own marital tragedy profoundly influenced his teaching. God would punish Israel, but it would be like that of a jealous lover, longing to bring back his beloved to the pure joy of their first love: 'I will betroth you to myself forever, betroth you with integrity and justice, with tenderness and love' (v. 21).

Isaiah

Isaiah (chs. 1–39), the greatest of the prophets, appeared in Judah towards the second half of the eighth century (740–700 BC) which witnessed the collapse of the northern kingdom of Israel (721 BC) and the attack on Jerusalem by the Assyrian army (701 BC).[4] His inaugural vision of the Lord enthroned in glory (6:1–13) left an indelible mark on Isaiah's ministry. The majesty, glory and holiness of the Lord gave him a new awareness of human depravity. The enormous distance between the holiness of God and human sinfulness overwhelmed him. Only after purification could he accept the call to prophecy which exposed the moral breakdown of Judah and its capital, Jerusalem (1:4–28; 3:1–17; 5:8'24).

Three convictions sum up his message: that the God of Israel, the Holy One, is truly in charge of all that is happening in the world; that the sinful condition of his people is so great that there is no hope of reform short of a devastating invasion by Assyria that will lay waste the towns and villages of his people; and that all is not lost, however, for a remnant will survive, and out of the ashes of this catastrophe a new people will be born (6:11–13).

Assyria's rise to power, however, was no accident of history. Behind it was the King of the universe (6:5) and Assyria would become his instrument (10:5). The coming Assyrian invasion, though, while inevitable and devastating, will not be total (9:1). The Assyrians themselves will be defeated because of their arrogance (10:13–16) and Jerusalem itself will be spared. This miracle of deliverance will bring about repentance and renewed faith (1:25–28) in a people involved in worshipping God through extravagant sacrifices while neglecting justice and care for the poor (1:10–20). Isaiah was particularly troubled by the arrogant attitude of Jerusalem's elite (2:6–5:25).

God is bringing the Assyrians to decimate Judah in order to humble its proud leaders, to purge Jerusalem of its sins, to demonstrate that God is indeed Lord of the universe, and to prepare the way for the advent of a new, more just leadership and community among the survivors, Isaiah explained. God's plan has relevance not only for social and religious affairs, but also for public policy. Since God himself is the ultimate power behind the rise of Assyria and its invasion of Israel, it would be folly to try to prevent its happening. What was called for instead was inner tranquillity and trust in the Lord (30:15). National survival and spiritual renewal lay, not in military might, but in conversion and tranquillity. King Ahaz, however, would not hear of it.

During the crisis of 732 BC, Jerusalem was threatened by an Israelite-Syrian coalition because it wished to replace King Ahaz of

Judah who had entered into an alliance with Assyria. Isaiah advised him to be calm and have no fear, to put his trust in God and things would turn out well. If he did not trust, he would not last (7:1–9). Isaiah's attitude is often misinterpreted. It is said that he was opposed to King Ahaz requesting help from Assyria. But what Isaiah opposes is the fear of the king and the people in the face of the crisis. The alternative is between faith and fear that presupposes a lack of trust in God who is obligated to Jerusalem and the Davidic dynasty by reason of the covenant with David (2 Sm 7). Isaiah's political stance was influenced by the religious traditions to which God had committed himself. But God's promises are not unconditional; they demand a response of faith manifested in an attitude of vigilance, calm and serenity in the knowledge that God will not fail to save his people. Opposed to this faith-attitude is seeking security based on foreign alliances and total dependence on foreign armies which leads not to security, but to fear and eventual disaster.

Since his preaching went unheeded for the most part, Isaiah entrusted his message to his disciples for preservation and transmission (8:16–20). The prophecies of Isaiah then moved from an appeal to Ahaz to a more responsive future king, a prince of peace who will rule over the remnant of Israel which has its nucleus in Isaiah and his disciples. From this period comes the messianic oracles (7:13–14; 9:5–6; 11:1–9). The word spoken by Isaiah, though unheeded by king and people alike, will form the order of a new community wherever it is heard and lived.

Jeremiah

Jeremiah, in the book that bears his name, combines history, biography and prophecy that introduce us to an extraordinary person who was totally identified with his prophetic office which began in 627 BC.[5] Jeremiah's life spanned a difficult period in religion, politics and war. It began with national independence and religious revival under Josiah (640–609 BC) and witnessed the downfall of Assyria and its replacement by Babylon. The unexpected death of Josiah brought about the collapse of his reform and precipitated the destruction of Jerusalem and Temple a short time later. The book portrays a nation in crisis due to its infidelity, which Jeremiah opposed with all his strength. This led to his arrest, imprisonment and public disgrace. He saw the nation's failure to repent as the sealing of its doom. Jerusalem was captured, the Temple was razed to the ground, king and nobles were carried off into exile in Babylon (587 BC). About this time, he uttered the great oracle of a new covenant, the climax of his teaching (31:31–34).

One of the most memorable events of Jeremiah's prophetic career was his Temple Sermon (7:1–15; 26:1–19). It was delivered at a time, probably on a feast-day, when throngs of people flocked to worship in the Temple. Jeremiah castigates them for the superstitious belief that the mere presence of God's Temple in their midst would be enough to protect them from their enemies irrespective of their conduct. In mantra-like fashion they chant: 'This is the temple of the Lord, the temple of the Lord, the temple of the Lord' (v. 4), while thinking that they are free to commit every kind of crime and abomination. The prophet calls for a radical change of lifestyle by citing prescriptions of the Decalogue. What he finds astonishing is that the people can go on violating its stipulations and continue worshipping in the Temple while claiming its protection like a security blanket. In these circumstances, the Temple is no longer a place of worship but a lair for robbers and will be destroyed like the shrine at Shiloh.

Jeremiah lays bare the anguish of his heart as he wrestles with God, confronts him with defiant questions, yet never doubts God's fidelity and concern. More than any other prophet, Jeremiah made himself the message. His laments (11:18–23; 12:1–6; 15:10–21; 17:14–18; 18:18–23; 20:7–13; 20:14–18) are examples of a highly personal understanding of his prophetic office that proclaims the divine word as it guides history. They portray Jeremiah as an example of one who suffered, yet is upheld by God's mercy. In this, he provides a model for the national suffering and vindication that awaited the whole nation. Jeremiah confronts the evil embodied in his enemies who sought to silence, imprison and even kill him. He struggles to understand how God could have left him alone to face enemies of the prophetic word, and becomes an example of one who himself is suffering divine judgment. His anguish will later become that of every Israelite. Jeremiah wanted to show the people how to suffer faithfully and not lose hope.

Jeremiah is the classic example of the rejected prophet. Despite the negativity of his message about the immediate prospects of his people, his view of the future is much more positive. The forgiveness of the people in the Sinai desert (Ex 34:9–10) served as a precedent for the announcement of a new covenant (31:31–34). Aware that the people had rejected the Sinai covenant, Jeremiah proclaimed that the people could keep it only if God changed their hearts (the seat of loyalty and devotion). In this way, they will be helped to respond to the divine word. The 'heart' will become the tablet on which the law of God will be written. Each person will be able to fulfil the original intention of the Sinai covenant that had become eclipsed by outward religious ceremonies and laws written on stone. Written upon the heart, the law will find expression in a personal response of obedience.

The character of Jeremiah is portrayed as one who lived and suffered for his faith. His life reflects the divine life as well; God is experienced not only in what Jeremiah says, but also in the word embodied in his life. It seems that the office of prophet increasingly invaded the personal and spiritual lives of individual prophets. With Amos the distinction is still clear; with Hosea and Isaiah prophetic office and private life begin to collapse; with Jeremiah this distinction is completely blurred. His prophetic office defines his person from the very beginning as the essence of his very being (1:4–10). He is shaped by God not only to be a certain kind of speaker, but also a certain type of person. Accordingly, he no longer has a private life; he must forego wife and children (16:1ff.) and the normal run of social activities (15:17). He has become the word of God embodied and becomes a vehicle of divine presence even while still retaining his distinct personality subject to all the flaws and foibles of a human being. Hence the prophet also embodies the suffering of God for his people.

Jeremiah suffered not only persecution, but also the anguish of knowing that his words were not being heeded (20:7–10). Among the prophets, Jeremiah becomes the lone spiritual personality who, more than any of the prophets, differentiated the right order of the soul from mere external behaviour. Right order comprised personal responsibility that included humility, right conduct, knowledge of God, fear of the Lord (awe, reverence) and love (*hesed*). His own life was in effect an 'enfleshment' of the life of God. The lamenting Jeremiah mirrors before the people the lamenting God in an effort to motivate them to repent. The tension in God over what to do with a rebellious people whom he loves has its counterpart in the life of the prophet. Jeremiah's task therefore was to portray in a living and personal fashion before the people the anguish of God. He was forced to spend his final days in Egypt cut off from his own people. In this way, the homelessness of the prophet embodied in a unique way the homelessness of God among his own people.

Ezekiel

Ezekiel, priest and prophet, was among the first batch of deportees exiled to Babylon in 597 BC.[6] He settled with the exiles in the transplanted community. Unlike his contemporaries, he saw the Exile as a long process of judgment that required faith and trust. His call and commission in chapters 1–3 describe a vision of divine glory that will depart from the Temple because of the sins committed within it, corrupted by cultic abominations and injustice (chs. 8–10). As well as preaching, Ezekiel employed visionary experiences and precise dating to remind readers that he was interpreting real events and urging his hearers to practical action. Although the scroll in his inaugural vision was filled with 'lamentation and wailing and woe' (2:10), his message is ultimately about a bright future that God has in store for his people. In chapters 40–48 he describes the new city and the new Temple. Holiness implied personal responsibility for social justice (18:1–32), and social justice in turn required right worship. For Ezekiel, Israel's sin consisted essentially in defiling the sanctuary through idolatry (chs. 8, 11). But before the new world could dawn, evil must first be purged and defeated.

Salvation is reserved for those in exile who have been transformed through repentance that will result in interior renewal: 'I will give you a new heart and put a new spirit in you ... and make you keep my laws and sincerely respect my observances' (36:26–27). The dry bones will be brought back to life (37:1–14). The prophet showed them the future so that they could endure, trust in God alone and hope for the world that God would bring about. God will provide a place where his people can hear and encounter him, a dwelling place among his people. The reason for the Lord acting thus was not because of Israel's virtues or miseries, but 'that they may know that I am the Lord' (used more than fifty times in

Ezekiel) – God acts because of who he is, and so the basis of hope is in God, not in human beings.

Second-Isaiah

Second-Isaiah (Is 40–55) preached in the middle of the sixth century BC to the exiles in Babylon to encourage them to return to Jerusalem.[7] The earlier phase of destruction and punishment was at an end and a new phase was about to begin (40:1–11). The prophet's pastoral task consisted in summoning the people to return and Cyrus, the pagan king of Persia, was to be God's instrument to bring it about. Engaging in a new exodus will bring Israel back to the promised land and show the nations that it is the Lord alone who determines the course of history.

His preaching includes four servant songs (42:1–9; 49:1–7; 50:4–11; 52:13–53:12) that refer not to Israel but to an individual whose identity remains obscure.[8] This mysterious figure fulfils the vocation of the people of Israel by proclaiming to the nations that Israel's exile and sufferings do not mean that God is ineffectual, but rather shows his justice and compassion. The fourth song especially is an extraordinary description of a sinless servant who by his voluntary suffering atones for the sins of the people and saves them from just punishment at the hands of God. Through his sufferings they are healed, and so redemption comes about as the fruit of his suffering: 'Ours were the sufferings he bore, ours the sorrows he carried … He was pierced through for our faults, crushed for our sins … and through his wounds we are healed' (53:4, 5).

It is the suffering of the faithful servant, not the political society, who represents the divine order and restores humankind. He is not named but his portrayal as an individual is so detailed as to approach the biographical. Unlike the Israelite people, he is not deaf or blind. He listens to God and submits in silence to his lot. The fourth song in particular influenced the portrayal of Jesus in the New Testament: 'For the Son of Man himself did not come to be served, but to serve, and to give his life as a ransom for many' (Mk 10:45). Jesus, through his death and resurrection, is the Suffering Servant who wrought salvation by freely offering his life out of love for humanity.

Anthropological Perspectives

To understand the prophetic message, we must begin with the earlier prophets. What provoked them to initiate a new religious revival, write down their prophecies and publicise them? They were convinced that the Lord's covenant relationship with Israel, which resulted in a distinctive way of living, had reached a crisis point. Added to this was the rise of new superpowers (Assyria, Babylon) against whom Israel was unable to defend herself. These two factors severely called into question the religious traditions, the national story (Pss.105, 124, 136) that proclaimed that the Lord had freed his people from slavery and given them the Promised Land in perpetuity. Political changes in the surrounding nations, however, had made the people's possession of the land precarious and uncertain. Israel's identity as God's special people was called into question and prophets were needed to re-interpret the ancient traditions to make it possible for the people to respond to this new situation.

Each prophet in his own way emphasised the centrality of the relationship to the Lord and guided the people to an appropriate response. Elijah called the people to decision; Amos exposed the rampant social injustice; Hosea used the prospect of a new exodus to exhort the people to remain faithful. Otherwise the much-awaited 'Day of the Lord' would mean the Lord's punishment of Israel rather than its enemies. Isaiah recovered forgotten aspects of the Jerusalem and Davidic traditions to show that God's promises of protection demanded fidelity on the people's part. Jeremiah utilised the exodus tradition to demonstrate that the sufferings the people were experiencing could have a positive outcome in a renewed covenant if the people were to become obedient. Ezekiel interpreted the historical events of his time from a priestly perspective in a renewed liturgy in a rebuilt Temple.

Prophets had a two-fold task: to interpret the national traditions in the light of the ever-changing course of history and to persuade the people to act in accord with the required changes. The prophets had to explain to the people that what was happening was the work of the Lord who was purifying his people. Jeremiah, for example, saw Babylon as God's instrument to purge Judah by destroying Jerusalem and the Temple and leading Israel captive to a foreign land.

The problem in daily living was incarnating the new order of the soul attuned to the will of God while living in the world. The Sinai covenant had created a new type of people with a new charter or constitution articulated in the Decalogue as the expression of the new order of living. Violations of the Decalogue uncovered the problems in Israelite society. In Jeremiah 7:1–15 people were coming to the Temple for security, yet they 'steal, murder, commit adultery, swear falsely'. The Decalogue's stipulations (5–10) helped to classify these social evils. The disorder in society could be judged on the basis of anti-God (idolatry) and anti-human (injustice) self-assertiveness, as lack of reverence for God and lack of respect for fellow Israelites when they failed to listen to the voice of God. Since the king no longer had spiritual authority, this gave rise to conflict between Israel as interpreted by the king and Israel as interpreted by the prophets (Jer 26). The prophetic preaching demanded a change of attitude and conduct that was not forthcoming; only a remnant will hearken to the prophets' call. Existence under God must also include positive elements like love, humility, trust and right conduct that must be internalised as the right order of the soul in openness to God and summed up in: 'Do justice, love kindness and walk humbly with your God' (Mic 6:8).

The cultivation of virtue expressed the spirit of the Decalogue which enabled one to become a certain type of person, rather than mere external ritualistic and legal observance. The preaching of the pre-exilic prophets therefore consisted for the most part of warnings to bring about a change of heart in order to avert catastrophe and re-attune the souls of the people to the divine order. For this, the prophets were attacked and abused; they suffered and were persecuted. Nevertheless, they succeeded in keeping alive the new order through schools of disciples which became carriers of the message. The true Israel, therefore, was no longer the historical, political Israel, but only a remnant who actually lived the covenant relationship. This meant suffering in solitude in communion with God as society at large headed towards destruction. Jeremiah, in his time, became the sole carrier of the new order. God was experienced as present not only in what Jeremiah said, but also in the word embodied in his life. The carriers of the divine order henceforth will be *individuals* who respond positively to the word of God and live in community as 'the faithful remnant'. They will carry the new order into the future in a new covenant (Jer 31:31–34), a renewed heart (Ez 36:26–28) and under a new leader (Messiah; Is 9:1–6, 11:1–9). He will embody the will of God, lead his transformed people to spread the good news of salvation to the nations who in turn will come to worship in the Temple in a holy pilgrimage (Is 2:2–5). Normally, a god who loses his land, allows his people to be defeated and his temple to be destroyed is a god who is overthrown and vanishes from history. In the case of Israel, the opposite happened. The faith of Israel deepened and reached its true form and stature. Their God had not abandoned his people in defeat. The God of Israel is also the Creator of the world who is known in some manner in all the religions. He it was who spoke to Abraham, who chose Israel, but who is also the God of all peoples who guides the course of history. He is Lord of the whole world. These insights found literary expression in the creation narratives at the beginning of Genesis.

Endnotes

1   Bernhard W. Anderson, Steven Bishop and Judith H. Newman, 'Prophetic Troublers of Israel', in *Understanding the Old Testament* (5th edn), New Jersey: Prentice Hall, 2007, pp. 248–255.

2   For further reading, see John W. Miller, *Meet the Prophets*, New York: Paulist Press, 1987. See also, Thomas L. Leclerc, *Introduction to the Prophets: Their Stories, Sayings and Scrolls*, New York: Paulist Press, 2007, and Gerhard von Rad, *The Message of the Prophets*, London: SCM Press, 1968.

3   Anderson *et al.*, 'Fallen is the Virgin Israel', *op. cit.*, pp. 267–289.

4   *Ibid.*, pp. 294–313.

5   *Ibid.*, pp. 356–385.

6   *Ibid.*, pp. 388–424.

7   *Ibid.*, pp. 425–459.

8   Eric Voegelin, *Order and History, vol. 1: Israel and Revelation (The Collected Works of Eric Voegelin, vol. 14)*, (M. Hogan, ed.), Columbia: University of Missouri Press, 2001, pp. 542–570.

CHAPTER EIGHT:
WISDOM LITERATURE

Introduction[1]

Our instinct to discern order within our world to keep chaos at bay is clearly expressed in the wisdom literature. Without an ordered cosmos, even science as we know it today would be impossible. The wisdom books are reflections on and interpretations of life as lived – an intellectual enterprise consisting of observed experiences and ethical claims expressed in artistic speech that is meant to persuade individuals to behave in a certain way. Their content is based on creation faith, a reflection on the world and human experience, a world that is ethically ordered, and this order is rooted in God's purposes. Wisdom, then, is the studied, reflected judgment about reality; how to live well, responsibly and happily for the world is a given with which one must come to terms. The sages valued all human experiences and linked them to the larger horizon of international reflection outside of Israel, based on the belief that the God of Israel presides over the life and death of their neighbours.

The wisdom tradition is preserved in a distinct section of the Old Testament comprising Proverbs, Sirach, Qoheleth, Job, and Wisdom of Solomon. Contemplating nature and reflecting on experience, the sages discovered that there are certain givens in life, certain laws that, if followed, would lead to enhancement of life, God's greatest gift. They were also concerned about human ethical behaviour, interpersonal relationships and accomplishment in work. They pondered as well the tragic in life – suffering, injustice, the mystery of evil, retribution and destiny. The ability to perceive an order in nature through reflection on life as lived and harmonise their lives in accordance with it became known as wisdom (*hokmah*). The sages, however, never believed that life could be completely understood or controlled, for life is bounded by mystery, cannot be fully fathomed, and can only be accepted. The wisdom that fully explains the universe is beyond human reach and resides in God alone, the all-wise (Job 28:1–28), an attribute personified to highlight its importance (Prov 8:22–31) and a gift to be prayed for (Wis 9:1–18).

The post-exilic period gave rise to this wisdom literature and to the spiritual movement that underpinned it. Wisdom takes its place alongside the Law and the Prophets. Here, the faith in the one God achieves greater depth. The literature links God to the world through wisdom and conceives the world as reflecting the rationality of its Creator. The connection is made between God and the world, between rational thought and revelation, which answers both the deepest religious longings and the requirements of reason that Greek philosophy had been groping for. Wisdom is concerned primarily with individuals, their relationships, their welfare, values and dignity. The wise person cultivates a flexibility of mind that enables one to respond appropriately to every concrete situation as it arises.

Despite similarities with the wisdom traditions of the surrounding cultures, Israelite wisdom is in accord with its faith in God. It is highly ethical and monotheistic, and includes fidelity to the law of Moses as a source of wisdom (Sir 24), which gave biblical wisdom a quality different from merely human wisdom. The 'fear of the Lord' became the basis of true wisdom – reverence, awe, trust and devotion to God that was shown in obedience and piety, for the sages were also worshippers. They believed that religious life is not limited to prayer and worship alone, but encompasses the details of daily life where myriads of smaller decisions are made, for there is no dichotomy between worship and daily living.

Proverbs

The Book of Proverbs is mostly a collection of short sayings known as proverbs for living a virtuous and fulfilling life. A composite work that was gathered together over time, Proverbs is attributed to Solomon, the wise man par excellence (1 Kgs 4:30–34), and so it anchors a predominantly secular wisdom in the covenant history of Israel. Reverence for God (Prov 1:7) becomes the foundation of a work that consists largely of observations and exhortations to live an upright life. The proverbs themselves are compressed, instructive statements, usually two-line sentences, but broad enough to include longer discourses. The goal of these instructions is not abstract philosophy or specialised knowledge for professional advancement alone; they guide above all in leading a virtuous and fulfilling life on a daily basis.

The Book of Proverbs' primary purpose is to teach wisdom. It begins with a lengthy introduction (chs. 1–9) commending the pursuit of wisdom while avoiding the dangerous seductions of vice. The proverbs are examples that are intended to instruct by inviting one to reflect on life as experienced. For example: 'A flood of words is never without its fault; he who has his lips controlled is a prudent man' (10:19, a warning against gossip); 'A city is raised on the blessing of honest men; it is demolished by the mouth of the wicked' (11:11, individual character determines the quality of social life); 'The simpleton believes what he is told; the man of discretion watches how he treads' (14:15, a warning against fake news!); 'Where reflection is wanting, zeal is not good; he who goes too quickly misses the way' (19:2, the danger of impetuosity); 'Iron is made finer by iron; a person is refined by contact with one's neighbour' (27:17, social intercourse develops character). By means of comparison and contrast, proverbs provide insights into the complexities of life so that one can discern appropriate ways of responding to what life throws up at them. The collection ends with an alphabetic poem extolling the virtues of a capable wife that is offered for imitation (31:10–31). The purpose of the collection is less to indoctrinate than to educate, less informative than formative.

The process, however, is more important than the product. Wisdom highlights the importance of reflection on experience and Proverbs provides examples and illustrations from which one can learn. It offers an appreciation of life and encouragement to live it to the fullest by being attentive to experience, reflective and intelligent in acquiring knowledge and insights into life, reasonable in judging their truthfulness, responsible in making decisions in the light of the truth discovered, and loving by fearing God and keeping his commandments, for we live in God's world that to us is often mysterious and unfathomable.

Sirach[2]

The Book of Sirach (Ecclesiasticus) is a synthesis of the entire tradition of wisdom in Israel as a bulwark against a decadent Greek culture that was invading Palestine in the wake of Alexander's conquests. The author also includes famous personalities from salvation history who exemplify wisdom, thereby forging a unity between God's work evident both in creation and in salvation history. Sirach succeeded in explicitly linking experiential wisdom to God's revelation in history, the law of Moses, Temple piety, ethical living and personal devotion, as well as offering exemplary models from salvation history (chs. 44–50) held up for encouragement and imitation. The book offers a recipe for the formation of a certain type of person comprising character, virtues, attitudes and deeds that in turn will form a certain type of society to ensure harmony and peace to preserve its distinctive lifestyle.

In Sirach, both revelation and experiential wisdom are explicitly brought together and integrated in a harmonious unity. From his meditation on the Hebrew scriptures as well as reflection on traditional wisdom, Sirach compiled his own notes, comments, and maxims which he edited and published in a new synthesis to serve the needs of his contemporaries who were tempted by the allurements of pagan (Hellenistic) culture around the turn of the second century BC. He does not offer a systematic presentation, but rather a series of reflections, exhortations and advice in no particular order.

The author sees human beings as free agents in a good world created by God, not hapless victims of fate, heredity or environment (15:11–20). As social beings, they have the possibility and responsibility of living happily and meaningfully (17:1–24). Made in the divine image, all peoples have the same dignity and abilities and struggle with the same limitations. They are endowed with knowledge, understanding and wisdom so that they can praise their Creator when they contemplate his magnificent works. Existentially, they suffer the limitations of creaturehood (40:1–11), especially when they misuse their freedom to sin. No one is spared the pain associated with the human condition. To psychological terrors are added external woes, a 'heavy yoke' from which nobody is exempt.

The Book of Sirach includes a whole range of topics that make for virtuous living and human fulfilment, providing thereby a kind of handbook for proper relationships and moral behaviour. Although wisdom finds its home in Israel (24:8–12) and is identified in part with the law of Moses (v. 23), wise and virtuous conduct is within reach of all since God from the beginning poured out his wisdom on all humanity (1:9–10; 24:6–7). Much of the content of Sirach consists of habits, attitudes and dispositions that enable one to become a certain type of person by forging appropriate relationships. There is a broad spectrum of virtues and vices for the cultivation of character; for example, humility, patience, sincerity, prudence, discretion, moderation, forgiveness, and self-control. Vices to avoid include pride, presumption, inappropriate speech, hypocrisy, resentment, inordinate sensual desires and unrestrained temper. These are universal in that they concern human beings everywhere. As well, there are duties to God, family and social life, rules of conduct and counsels for a variety of concrete circumstances. No situation in life is unworthy of attention, for humans can discover the Creator in daily living, which is primarily the domain of traditional wisdom.

Sirach offers the possibility of developing a well-rounded life that includes a religious and moral dimension, the marks of a mature character. A person of character has a certain integrity, a wholeness or completeness which is the aim and goal of biblical wisdom. Because of its universal outlook, Israelite wisdom literature may provide a model for understanding revelation other than from a salvation history viewpoint. In it, dialogue with God takes place through experience of his creation that is also available to other peoples – a faith mediated through creation. The Creator revealed in creation is also the Saviour of Jews and Christians. It is Christ as Wisdom Incarnate who makes possible a faith engendered by experience of God's creation in a way accommodated to each person's spiritual situation.

Sirach achieved a new synthesis of religion and culture which embraces creation and humanity, history and wisdom, a *Weltanschauung* (worldview) for his contemporaries to make sense of their beliefs. There is no dichotomy between sacred and profane. His God is a God of all people who works in a special way in Israelite history but is not confined within it. Divine wisdom is operative both in creation and in salvation history. The wisdom literature of Israel can also serve to re-establish links between faith and culture, enabling one to live an authentic human life in an integrated system of beliefs, values, customs and in institutions that express them. In this way, it provides the glue that binds society together to give a sense of identity, security and continuity to people when transcendent values and the dignity of the individual are both recognised and promoted.

Qoheleth[3]

The Book of Qoheleth (Ecclesiastes) is a loose collection of sayings, observations and admonitions flowing from life as lived and reflected on. It includes tensions and apparent contradictions that must be kept in balance if one is to appreciate its message. An Israelite sage reflects on the meaning of life's ambiguities as they impinge on human living. No discernible order, it seems, governs the universe, for God acts mysteriously in ways unknown to human beings. The author struggles with the futility of life seen against the inevitability and universality of death. His critical approach offers an outlook on life that is relevant for human beings at all times and in all places.

Content

After a few introductory sentences, the author paints a picture of a world full of activity (1:4–11). Yet, despite all the goings-on, nothing much happens in the end. The world as humans experience it is an unchanging stage on which the drama of natural and human activity takes place. No advantage is gained despite all the activity; even human toil yields no progress. Human beings come and go, and each generation must begin again. This, Qoheleth says, is 'vanity'.

Continuing his theme (1:12–3:15) and donning the mantle of Solomon, the author tells us that even a wise and powerful ruler, despite all the opportunities available to him, comes away from life empty-handed, for nothing in life is permanent. The advantages of wisdom are limited since in the face of death both the wise and the foolish are equal. Whatever material gain – wisdom, pleasure, success – that is acquired through human effort must be relinquished; nothing can change the fact that death is the fate of every human being. In the light of this truth, people can only enjoy the good things given to them by God as a gift. Humans are not in control. Only God is in charge. For order in the world is elusive – things occur at a time that God determines. Even though humans have an intuition of the eternal (ʿolam, 3:11), they can only live in the here and now and so all vain speculation is futile.

Qoheleth proceeds to give some glimpses of the social conditions in which humans live out their lives (3:16–6:10). There is corruption in the administration of justice, exploitation, rivalry, unstable and incompetent leadership, covetousness, greed and bankruptcy. How is one to conduct oneself in these situations? The author suggests a proper attitude towards God (4:17–5:9) that emphasises divine transcendence and counsels caution and restraint in the practice of religion. Furthermore, people must not brood over their miseries, rather they should accept the gift of joy whenever it presents itself.

In 6:11–9:6, the author reflects on major themes of classical wisdom teaching in order to critique them. Since God alone is in control of all that happens, humans are not in a position to challenge or change the nature of things that God has made. They can only accept what God does. Nor can they know what will happen in the future, for this knowledge eludes them. Even wisdom and righteousness are elusive. The traditional doctrine of retribution is contradicted by experience, for things do not always turn out as expected. The only alternative is to accept human limitations and that life includes good and evil. For the reality is that righteous people are often treated as if they were wicked, and wicked people as if they were righteous. This situation is beyond human comprehension, for people live in a seemingly arbitrary world which they neither control nor understand. Death is the fate of all mortals regardless of their character, and so it is best to leave everything in God's hands.

For this reason, the author counsels living life to the full (9:7–12:7), for in death no one will have the opportunity to accomplish anything. Since there is no fail-safe formula in life, practical wisdom, although not a formula for success, will achieve some benefit. Because there are all sorts of political, social and economic forces at work in society, wisdom may reduce the risks which can never be completely eliminated. Nevertheless, there are times in which one must take risks, for over-cautiousness will never achieve anything and life means participation. Remembering the days to come prompts one to enjoy life while one is able, before life draws to a close and humanity goes to its eternal home. This marks the end of life as humans experience it. Qoheleth ends with an appropriate conclusion which is the thematic statement of the book – all is vanity. An epilogue endorses the orthodoxy of its content. His reflections may be summed up: 'What does it profit a man to gain the whole world and forfeit his life?' (Mk 8:37).

Anthropological Perspectives

The author begins with a thematic statement that frames his book: "'Vanity of vanities," says Qoheleth, "Vanity of vanities. All is vanity"' (1:2; 12:8). The word 'vanity' (*hebel*), which is mentioned thirty-eight times throughout the book, suggests what is ephemeral and insubstantial, but also what is incomprehensible and mysterious. In the body of the book, the author offers evidence that led him to this conclusion. Given that humans live in a world where everything is transient and fleeting, Qoheleth offers advice on how to conduct oneself in such a predicament. Nothing that human beings achieve can alter the fact of death, nor do they know what will happen afterwards. Events in life happen at a time that God decides; he alone is in charge and mortals are in no position to challenge the divine management of the world or to alter the nature of things. That order exists in the world, Qoheleth never doubts, but this order does not conform to human standards. In the face of the manifest inequalities of life, some things enable one to better cope with life, yet even these are of relative value only.

Qoheleth parts company with his predecessors who were overly optimistic that the wise and virtuous always prosper while the foolish and wicked suffer. The experience of living and observation of human conduct, he says, shows that the opposite is not infrequently the case and that injustice in human affairs too often prevails. The reality of good and evil in life must be accepted. People try to cope with this situation in various ways. They work hard, accumulate wealth and hoard it, and pursue wisdom and understanding; they even attempt to straighten what is crooked, correct injustice, try to gain immortality through fame, wealth or accomplishments. They endeavour in every conceivable way to gain control of a situation, but nothing really works. The only viable alternative is to accept that nothing can be fully controlled by humans and let go. When they recognise what is really happening in their world, they have the freedom to accept joyfully both the possibilities and the limitations of the human condition at every given moment.

For despite all the anomalies of life, there is the possibility of finding joy, pleasure and contentment in all one does. Seven times Qoheleth explicitly exhorts people to enjoy life whenever opportunities present themselves (2:24–26), as an antidote to life's miseries (5:18, 20) and as a gift from God (3:12–13). One should enjoy life as one progresses from youth to old age (11:9; 12:1), yet nowhere does he advocate a hedonistic lifestyle.

The transcendent God is not withdrawn from the world he created. He is constantly active both in the world and in human life (2:26; 3:11) although his workings remain a mystery. He judges the just and the wicked (3:17), but Qoheleth admits he doesn't know when or how. Human life is ultimately in God's hands and so we must learn to accept, appreciate and enjoy what is within our grasp. For human life is in the living of it, and human endeavour has merit only to the extent that it enhances a quality of life.

Towering above all life's uncertainties looms the spectre of death, the one thing in life that is inevitable and inescapable. Death comes to everybody irrespective of character or achievement. Although death is certain, its timing is uncertain; it may come whether one is ready or not. Death marks the end of life for the author, for nobody knows for sure what happens after death (3:21). At the time of death, the body returns to the earth, while the life-breath returns to God (12:7).

In face of the uncertainty of life, Qoheleth inculcates a different kind of character formation and offers his own list of attitudes and virtues to cultivate it. The basic attitude is 'fear of the Lord' (3:14), that is, the cultivation of devotion and loyalty to God. This is the proper response to a transcendent God who acts in mysterious ways in the world. It also includes humility to embrace one's creaturely status as well as acknowledging in a spirit of gratitude the blessings bestowed by God. He questions the adequacy of traditional character formation with its unquestioned appropriation of the accumulated wisdom of the past. It is in the quest itself that the contours of character are shaped when one accepts the vicissitudes of life together with moments of joy in humble and grateful acceptance as God's gift. In this way, life is lived without pretentions or delusions. Qoheleth transcends the ethos of entitlement and grievance in favour of unconditional acceptance of life on its own terms.

Qoheleth holds up to view what human beings are inclined to ignore, disguise or deny (death, undeserved suffering, injustice, chance, the anomalies of life, etc.) or alternatively embellish (work, wisdom, righteousness, success, wealth, knowledge, prestige, pleasure, etc.) and invites us to return to reality. His scepticism is not about the realities of life, nor about the existence of God or his providence, but about all doctrines, ideologies, beliefs and practices by which people delude themselves into thinking that they have found the ultimate meaning of life and so can control their destiny. Qoheleth is the great guardian of truth, for which he searches with passion while acknowledging the mystery of life and the transcendent God who acts with sovereign freedom both in the world and in human history. It is within these parameters that life is to be lived and that attitudes, habits and behaviour appropriate to such an outlook are to be developed.

Qoheleth shows the bankruptcy of a world-immanent rationality to resolve the deeper issues of life and death but remains open to the good news of eternal life (3:21). An editor commends Qoheleth as a wisdom teacher (12:9–13) who taught in a provocative way, prodding people out of their comfort zones to reflect on the fleetingness of life, the inevitability of death and the meaning of it all. His reflections are still relevant in a secularised world of technology that seeks to eliminate faith in a God who rules the world. What remains is a silent, empty and lonely world that eventually leads to nihilism and despair. Qoheleth's reflections, on the other hand, take God's existence and providential care for granted, and remain open to the solution of life's enigmas provided by revelation.

Job[4]

Content

Despite its length and the complexity of its contents, with possible additions (chs. 32–37) and misplacements (chs. 25–27), a skeletal outline of the Book of Job can aid in determining how it is to be read. A prose narrative frames the poetic section (chs. 1–2; 42:7–17) and sets the scene for the reader by presenting the human tragedy of an innocent and virtuous man (Job) who is struck down by loss and suffering. Two poetic sections follow: in the first, Job reacts by engaging in discussion with three minor characters (chs. 3–31); in the second, God responds in a theophany (chs. 38–41). The two major characters in this drama are Job (Everybody) and God, each presenting a point of view on the world and the human situation. The primary concern of the author is to isolate, point up and mirror for the reader an aspect of reality as experienced by human beings so that they become involved in the search for the meaning of it all.

To achieve this aim, the author places before the reader two contrasting options: a human viewpoint (Job and his friends) in the dialogue and God's view of the same situation in the theophany. In this way, a human tragedy is exposed that elicits two contrasting responses. What answer the book contains comes indirectly from the author's vision of the human predicament that includes the experience of evil and mindless suffering.

The prose prologue portrays an ethical and religious profile (1:1,8; 2:3) of a man, a friend of God and showered with blessings, who is struck down by tragedy. It is God who allows Job to suffer and may very well be the cause (1:12; 2:6; 42:11). The question about motivation for piety (self-interest or disinterested love) is raised as well as the kind of God with whom humans have to deal are raised for the reader to contemplate.

Job's dispute with his friends begins with a lament (ch. 3) about the human condition, then moves on to an attack on the traditional theology of retribution espoused by his friends and from there to an indictment of God himself. For the human condition leads inevitably to the problem of God. The friends' explanation does not fit the reality of innocent suffering, yet claims to determine it. To Job, God appears as arbitrary and cruel (chs. 6–7) and may even be guilty of injustice (9:22). This prompts him to demand a trial scene for God to explain himself (13:22) but to no avail, for God cannot be found (23:8–9). Nevertheless, Job continues his complaint, accusing God of presiding over a disordered world to which, apparently, he is deaf and blind (ch. 24). For Job, God and his ways are beyond human comprehension and unacceptable. To his friends, Job is proposing a strange theology by arguing from experience rather than tradition and they are forced to dismiss it as heretical. So great is Job's trust in his own innocence that he challenges God to recognise the innocence of his friend (ch. 31). The dialogue ends in stalemate.

Job challenged God to appear and respond to his accusations. God does appear but, instead of responding, he confronts Job with a barrage of questions in three blocks of poetry: cosmological (chs. 38:2–38), creational (38:39–39:30), and chaotic (40:15–41:34). Job stands revealed as incapable of fathoming the mystery of creation and coping with its chaos. The structure of the drama, however, cannot be allowed to end with Job's submission (42:1–6). An epilogue (42:7–17) rounds off the poetic section and describes Job's restoration as a fitting end to the book's argument.

Anthropological Perspectives

What kind of God allows an innocent man to suffer for no apparent reason? And this God is the Creator of the world and the Saviour of Israel! The function of the dialogue between Job and his friends is to oppose the notion of a comprehensible God to one that is numinous and transcendent. This leads to an appreciation of the mystery of God and his dealings with the world. By this time in Israel, the doctrine of retribution had become a complacent and mechanical theology that allowed an unexamined tradition to determine the whole of reality. The author maintains that the human existential situation leads to a desire to reach beyond the world and touch the transcendent. To do this, one must first have one's certainties about God and his dealings with his creation shattered, for what happens in the life of human beings comes about without regard to good or evil. That is why suffering and prosperity must be viewed differently from the prevailing theodicy enunciated by the friends.

At the conclusion of the dialogue, the reader is left with a God who is not tied to the canons of human justice and who acts beyond what human reason is able to cope with. God is transcendent, mysterious and incomprehensible; his ways of dealing with the world and human beings are not reducible to the traditional ways of thinking. It is Job alone who emerges from the discussion with enhanced dignity despite his emotional outbursts and wild accusations; his friends have been silenced and discredited.

Job had challenged God to appear. He is hoping for a dramatic encounter that would prove God wrong and he himself innocent. The reader perhaps is hoping for an intellectual answer to the problem of innocent suffering and by now has identified with Job against his friends. However, without a counter argument of some kind, the reader would be left with a cold, unfeeling and cruel God. God's questioning of Job reveals that he is incapable of fathoming the mystery of creation and coping with its chaos. He comes to the realisation that in the universe there is a mysterious harmony that includes chaos and evil, which are nevertheless controlled by God. Job is made aware of his essential limitations; his knowledge is inadequate to control or even make sense of his environment. Furthermore, his powerlessness in the face of the chaos that forms part of life is beyond his control, but not God's. Job is satisfied that he can trust God in his dealings with the world and is now free to love or not to love.

God's speeches hardly represent a response to Job's queries. They do not refute his arguments or resolve the issues he raised. In fact, they are not even mentioned. His speeches rather present another viewpoint on the universe and humans' place in it. Without this alternative viewpoint, the reader would not be forced to reassess his presuppositions regarding the universe and the God who created it. God's questioning of Job is meant to aid the reader in his own independent thinking and to arrive at his own conclusions. They are not an 'answer' to the problem of innocent suffering as such (which is not even mentioned), nor to the absurdity of the human condition in general. By means of interrogation, God makes Job see the same familiar world in different colours by placing certain experiences before him and invites him to draw his own conclusions.

The reader is also challenged to question his assumptions and stereotypes and face reality. It is essential that no simplistic solution be offered. For order in the universe transcends human understanding and allows God to be incomprehensible and transcendent. Human understanding is partial and incomplete as befits creatures. There is mystery at the heart of the universe and human beings must choose how to respond to it. Job and his friends are both right and wrong and the reader is unsure what God is revealing in his speeches. One thing is certain: God cannot be fully comprehended either by traditional categories or by those born of experience. Both are limited and must be expanded and balanced within a broader perspective. No one image of God is adequate to communicate the reality of the true God. The Book of Job, therefore, serves as a necessary corrective to the ever-present temptation to create God in our own image and likeness. The biblical God is totally other, yet involved in his creation in ways that humans do not fully comprehend.

There is mystery at the heart of existence, while human life is of necessity contingent and limited. What endows it with value is the way one *chooses* to respond to it. Human beings are free to love or not to love God, whose nature is self-transcendent. God's answer to Job's persistent desire for a relationship may be viewed as an answer to anybody who is prepared to reach out for communion with the transcendent God.

> Never before Job, one might suggest, has the understanding of the depth of the capacity of a free humanity for participation in a universally loving other been so explicitly explored and expressed.[5]

The Lord's appearance exposed the ineluctable limits of Job's perspective and the inevitable self-preoccupation in the face of suffering.

Life after Death

As mentioned previously, from the dawn of history human beings have honoured their dead and maintained contact with them by burial rituals, care of tombs, even offerings placed on the tombs of their dead. According to the beliefs of primitive peoples, death was never regarded as total annihilation. While the body was interred in the earthen grave, something of the dead person persisted in the abode of the dead (Hades, Sheol, Gehenna, etc.), conceived in a very rudimentary fashion. All the dead shared the same miserable lot and once the gates of Sheol were entered, there was no return. The Old Testament people remained at this level of belief until a rather late date and waited for a clear revelation of the mystery of the afterlife. Before the inevitable onset of death, life was seen as fragile, a mere shadow (Wis 2:2). Death was sensed as an inimical force whose approach was suspected in every sickness and danger (Ps. 88:4ff; 18:5; 69:15ff; 116:3). Death and Sheol are powers already at work in this world and life becomes the anguished struggle against them because they contradict our natural desire to live. Human beings instinctively regard death as a penalty for sin (Gn 2:17; 3:19); it was not God's doing (Wis 1:13). God created humans to be incorruptible; death only entered through the envy of the devil (Wis 2:23) and manifests the presence of sin in the world.

The godless person is already on a slippery slope (Ps 73:18ff) whose final lot will be forever among the dead (Wis 4:19). But what about the death of the just? How can the death of the innocent be justified? (Ps 49:10). Both the pessimism of Qoheleth and the anguish of Job gave voice to this dilemma. The solution to this mystery required light from above for it is not within the power of human beings to save themselves from death. Already the psalmist expressed a hope, however vague: that God will not abandon his soul to Sheol (16:10); that God will redeem his soul from the clutches of Sheol (49:6); and that a relationship of love in this life between the just and God will persist beyond death (73:23–24). This hope will ultimately expand to immortality (Wis 2:23). Late Old Testament revelation announced the definitive deliverance and the ultimate triumph of God over death.

When God's kingdom is definitively established, the just who sleep in the dust will rise from their graves to participate in it forever, while the wicked will remain eternally in the grip of Sheol (Dn 12:2). The hope expressed in the psalms will become a reality when the just will be taken into glory and the virtuous will live forever (Wis 5:1–3, 15). The Maccabean martyrs could heroically bear their torments and bravely face death (2 Mac 7:9, 14, 23) because their hope was full of immortality (Wis 3:4). That is why prayers were offered for the dead (2 Mac 12:43ff).

The Wisdom of Solomon[6]

The Wisdom of Solomon addressed the query posed by Qoheleth (3:21) in chapters 1–5. There is life after death for those who pursue *dikaiosyne* (justice, virtue, love), the fruit of wisdom, for a loving relationship with God is everlasting and transcends physical death. On the other hand, a life of injustice severs that relationship and ends in both physical and spiritual death (1:12). Physical death for the just, therefore, becomes the beginning of a new life with God, while for the unjust, the prospect of death renders life meaningless.

The author presents his message by contrasting appearance and reality. The wicked mask their despair by means of pleasure-seeking lives, striving for power and violence towards the just who are a reproach to their way of living (2:1–20). By chance people are born and death is the end. Their reflections bear an uncanny resemblance to the secularist's worldview that is so much in evidence today. But what if physical death does not have the last word? For God did create human beings for immortality which is attained through virtuous living (1:15; 2:23). The death of the just is for them the beginning of a blissful existence. Tested and purified through suffering, they are now at peace and abide in God's love, for there is continuity of personal existence (3:1–9). 'The souls of the righteous are in the hand of God, and no torment will ever touch them ... but they are at peace' (3:1, 3). Although the author uses Greek terminology, his anthropology is Jewish. Soul in Greek is feminine, but the author says those *persons* (*hoi de* – masculine) are at peace. There is continuity of personal existence.

The contrast between appearance and reality is further heightened from the perspective of a final judgment scene (4:20–5:23). The sombre account of God's judgment becomes the negative motive for the author's exhortation to love justice and seek God while there is still time. A death worse than mortality awaits the wicked, which they have brought on themselves through their words and deeds. The just, in contrast, confidently stand before their oppressors who confess their guilt and, belatedly, realise the vacuity of their former lives. The just are counted among God's children and claim their lot among the saints. Victorious over death, they enjoy life with God forever, while the unjust are condemned and punished. Responsibility for greatness or for tragedy ultimately resides in the concrete choices of human beings.

Anthropological Perspectives

The living order of Israel had been buried beneath a theory of retribution, namely, that the good are rewarded and evil is punished in mechanical fashion in this life. Qoheleth and Job burst out of this straitjacket. Both lived their faith without dishonesty or illusion in the face of senseless chaos. They wrestled with hope and despair, light and darkness, order and chaos. Both tried to capture experiences which had to do with the relationship of the individual to his surrounding reality, including God.

The narratives of Genesis 1–11 and the language of wisdom were retained in the Old Testament to articulate profound human experiences. The destiny of human beings and the meaning of existence in God's plan is seen as a journey with the whole of creation towards fulness of life with God. But traversing this journey gives rise to problems and questions that are difficult to reconcile with the hope born of faith. This is particularly true of the presence of evil in the world. Evil committed leads to a just exile, expulsion from the garden of paradise. This is represented by the adamic narrative which highlights human responsibility for sin (Gn 3). But there is also evil undergone as in the case of innocent suffering. The Book of Job attempts to grapple with this aspect of evil. In a world ruled by a good and just God, suffering and evil emerge as enigmas when the demands of human justice can no longer explain them. In the end, Job experiences himself in relationship with the Creator, the source of life and of all that exists, and penetrates beyond an ethical vision to a deeper dimension of faith. Only in God are all the contradictions of life resolved existentially, but this God is a God who remains hidden.

The ordeal of the Servant in Second Isaiah makes suffering or evil undergone an action capable of redeeming the evil that is committed (sin). Suffering expiates the sins of the people (Is 53:4–5, 8) and so can have meaning by voluntary consent. In the Old Testament, the mystery of evil and suffering is placed within a world oriented to life. Within that framework, suffering can have value for life.

Adam symbolises evil committed; Job, evil that is undergone; the Suffering Servant, by his voluntary acceptance of suffering though innocent, symbolises suffering which expiates the evil committed. Suffering, then, becomes a gift which atones for the sins of the people. Already as a result of the experience of the Exile, sickness, death and abandonment are understood as vicarious suffering (Is 53), as well as punishment for sin. Suffering for God's sake and for others can be meaningful when it is voluntarily embraced.

In the psalms, during the course of the post-exilic period, the personal wrestling with God regarding the meaningfulness of their own spirituality led pious Israelites to entertain the hope that they would not be given up to Sheol, the abode of the dead, but would be in God's presence in the fulness of joy (Ps 16). Psalm 73 is an expression of existential anguish over the happiness of sinners, secure in their good fortune and apparently successful and content. The temptation of the psalmist was to become envious and wish to live like them. Piety seemed meaningless since there was no connection between action and destiny. The psalmist, however, received an illumination in the Temple in his contemplation of God (vv. 23–24). He realised that the happiness of the wicked is short-lived, an illusion in fact, and that the envious person is a fool. He came to appreciate the treasure he already had – his deeply experienced communion with God that is capable of overcoming even death itself. This certitude comes from personal experience, not from external sources. It derives from the Israelite concept of God and the idea of communion with him, making it unthinkable that 'this-worldliness' would have the last word. A new level of insight was gained in the experience of pious individuals in Israel.

Towards the end of the Old Testament period, through the experience of persecution and martyrdom, faithful Israelites came to a new assurance of life and a new way of confronting death (Dn 12:2; 2 Mac 7:1–42; Wis 3:1–9). The desire for immortality arises from the experience of love and communion with God and so the mystery of life is identical with the mystery of love. Death is met by going out of oneself and giving oneself to another. For God is God of the living, not of the dead. Life is God's gift which opens up new possibilities. It is more than material well-being and is found in truth and justice and includes suffering to discover the fulness of life.

The faith of Israel as portrayed in the wisdom literature and later works demonstrates the harmony between God and the world, between reason and mystery. It also gave moral guidance for daily living. But this universal God was still linked to a particular people and its particular way of life connected with Temple worship. A non-Jew could not become a member since membership was bound up with physical descent from Abraham. Only with the advent of Christianity did the breakthrough actually take place in Jesus who has 'broken down the wall between Jew and Gentile' (Eph 2:14).

Endnotes

1   For more in-depth studies, see: James L. Crenshaw, *Old Testament Wisdom: An Introduction,* Atlanta: John Knox, 1981; Roland E. Murphy, *The Tree of Life,* New York: Doubleday, 1990; Gerhard von Rad, *Wisdom in Israel,* London: SCM Press, 1972; Bruce C. Birch, Walter Brueggemann, Terence E. Fretheim and David L. Peterson, *A Theological Introduction to the Old Testament,* Nashville: Abingdon Press, 2005, pp. 381–424. For further reading, see the following notes.

2   Daniel J. Harrington, *Jesus Ben Sira of Jerusalem,* Collegeville, Minnesota: Liturgical Press, 2005.

3   Choon-Leong Seow, *Ecclesiastes,* The Anchor Bible, New York: Doubleday, 1997. Norbert Lohfink, *Qoheleth,* Minneapolis: Fortress Press, 2003.

4   Norman C. Habel, *The Book of Job: A Commentary,* OTL, Philadelphia: Westminster, 1985. See also, Robert Gordis, *The Book of God and Man,* Chicago: Chicago University Press, 1965; H.H. Rowley, *The Book of Job,* Grand Rapids: Eerdmans, 1976.

5   Brendan Purcell, *The Drama of Humanity: Towards a Philosophy of Humanity in History,* Frankfurt am Main: Peter Lang, 1996, p. 162.

6   David Winston, *The Wisdom of Solomon,* The Anchor Bible, New York: Doubleday, 1999.

CHAPTER NINE:
A WORSHIPPING COMMUNITY

Leviticus[1]

The Israelites understood their history as one of partnership with God in a historical drama. Their God had entered into a covenant relationship with them at Sinai and this resulted in a permanent dwelling of God among them in his Temple. He was not only their God, but God in their midst, Emmanuel, 'God-with-us'. Hence the detailed description of the construction of the sanctuary and its ministers (Ex 25–31, 35–40) as a place consecrated exclusively for worship, where liturgies and feasts were celebrated. The book of Leviticus, placed at the centre of the Pentateuch, defines Israelite liturgical life and practice. Chapters 1–16 detail how to approach God properly – laws for sacrifice and proper respect for foods and bodily functions, anointing of priests as mediators and major feasts. There is an emphasis on holiness and respect for the divine presence. Chapters 17–25 list the moral and ethical laws and ritual requirements for social and communal life as well as worship to inculcate a proper attitude towards God and respect for fellow Israelites.

The ritual prescriptions were meant to separate the sacred from the ordinary by setting apart a certain place and certain days, and by the rite of priestly consecration which created mediators who offered sacrifice on behalf of the people. The laws of purity involved those areas that touched the mystery of life and so must be respected and regulated. For example, animals without blemish were to be offered in sacrifice; diseases that indicated a loss of vitality made one unworthy to participate in the liturgy. The Day of Atonement (ch. 16) healed defilements and uncleanliness to ensure a proper approach to the all holy and transcendent God for the whole community. The ethical requirements helped people to positively relate to God by removing obstacles and included social obligations as well: 'You shall love your neighbour as yourself' (19:18). All of these requirements and laws were in function of facilitating a total commitment and dedication to God to live as his people: 'Be holy because I am holy' (Lev 11:45). The blessings and curses (Lev 26) called on the people to choose; obedience brings blessings, disobedience brings curses, and so there were consequences arising from one's actions. These laws were to be internalised out of love for the Lord to ensure a happy and prosperous life. The prophets helped to clarify what existence under God entailed in the personal and social spheres of life. The sages further specified what human existence in the world demanded, particularly that of the individual in the face of the mystery of life in day-to-day living. In this way, Israel discovered the meaning of its historical drama as the epiphany of God.

1, 2 Chronicles, Ezra, Nehemiah[2]

These books were written to encourage Judeans in their task of rebuilding the Temple and restoring national life in the immediate post-exilic period. There is emphasis on David as a liturgical reformer. It was he who brought the Ark to Jerusalem and enhanced the sacred liturgy with choirs and music that made the Temple, later built by Solomon, a divinely instituted place of worship. The returned exiles were thus reassured that God's saving plan was still on-going, and so they may expect God's support in their efforts to rebuild national life centred on worship of the Lord.

The significance of worship under the direction of priests and Levites for Israelite life was crucial. Accordingly, David is idealised as the founder and sponsor of the Jerusalem Temple and of the worship that was carried out there. The story of Solomon deals exclusively with the building of the Temple as envisioned by David. The Temple, with its rituals and priesthood, was the one lasting contribution of the Davidic monarchy. Once the Temple was rebuilt and the proper form of its liturgy restored, the essential elements of Jewish life, together with its law, were in place.

Psalms³

The Israelite people kept alive their distinctive way of life as they waited in hope for the Lord to send them a Saviour-Messiah. Conscious of being in partnership with God, they knew themselves to be called to respond to the divine presence. Not only did they regard their history as a dramatic narrative of God's deeds, they also addressed God in a very personal way. They sang hymns of praise. They complained to God in the depths of their distress. They thanked him for his graciousness towards them. The finest example of this conversation with God is found in the Psalter which lies at the heart of the lived faith of the Old Testament people. The psalms were appropriated by the worshipping community as a fitting and public expression of their faith. They include psalms of praise, thanksgiving, petition and trust and embrace all of human life, all human sentiments and emotions and the whole area of religious psychology. Through the psalms, the mystery of humanity as the counterpart of God is disclosed in an intimate and loving way.

Psalm 139 is a meditation on God's loving care for each person, the result of a concrete experience on the part of the psalmist. The divine 'You' knows 'me' with the intimate knowledge characteristic of persons, a relationship of love (*yadah*, used seven times, denoting fulness). The psalmist is conscious of being loved unconditionally by a God who is fully aware of all his actions, thoughts and words and this evokes sentiments of awe and admiration. His life is accessible to God at all times and places, and the protective hand of God guards him. In this way, God's loving care for the individual is highlighted. For human life is regarded not only as a natural, biological occurrence; it is also the result of the will and operation of a benevolent Creator working with the cooperation of human parents. God has intricately knit the psalmist in his mother's womb with an attention to detail similar to that of a weaver tracing a pattern. His whole life belongs to God – from the first moment of conception, through gestation and birth up to the present moment. Even his lifespan is already determined and noted down by God. His origin and destiny rest with God. Awareness of this evokes wonder, admiration, praise and thanksgiving for 'In him we live and move and have our being' (Acts 17:28).

The psalm articulates how God is revealed so that the engendering experience can be re-enacted by readers as they contemplate the presence of God in their own lives. First of all, through an awareness of his omniscience and omnipresence, and, secondly, through his marvellous shaping of each individual person with attention and loving care. It is God who gives life, dignity, self-worth and purpose to each individual. Each person is unique and custom-made, not mass-produced. Only after meditating on the full range of God's goodness and action does the psalmist comprehend his own place in the world and the malice of human wickedness, which evokes outrage on his part. He invites God to take care of it and to scrutinise his own heart to ensure upright living that will lead to his destination, to be with God for all eternity.

Psalm 104 is an exquisite articulation of faith in creation seen as the subject of personal experience and observation which provides motives for praise. There is a description of the variety, splendour, majesty, orderliness, symmetry and harmony of so many good things that sustain living creatures and human beings and are kept in existence by a benevolent Creator. This experience evokes a burst of spontaneous wonder, gratitude and praise for a world that is well looked after. Psalm 136 is a solemn prayer of thanksgiving celebrating the many expressions of God's goodness both in creation and in history. It unfolds in the form of a litany with the refrain 'for his steadfast love endures forever'. God's providence continues to provide for all living things (v. 25). Psalm 51 is a heartful prayer for cleansing, pardon and renewal. It begins with a confident appeal for mercy followed by a confession of sinfulness, requests for absolution and renewal, a vow to praise God and offer the sacrifice that God desires, namely, a self-offering. Only then is God pleased with the liturgical actions in a renewed Temple worship.

As we have seen, the covenant relationship was the Old Testament's centre of gravity. However, as time went on, violations of the covenant were so commonplace that the prophets sensed that a return to right order through conversion was practically impossible. Accordingly, as we have seen, Isaiah entrusted his message to his disciples who formed the remnant of the faithful Israel (Is 8:16–18), Zephaniah further identifies them with the 'anawim, the poor, to whom he opposes the proud (Zeph 2:3; 3:11–13). The Exile meant the end of Israel as a political entity, but it also marked the beginning of a spiritual rebirth, due in no small part to the prophets of the Exile. The fundamental traits of the pious Israelite are given expression in the psalms in a well-defined picture of devout and fervent souls contrasted with the wicked and sinners that was incarnated and lived by anonymous people during the centuries following the Exile.

The faithful remnant who now take the name of the 'poor of Yahweh' carry on the traditions of the prophets and their voice can be heard in the psalms. Known as *tehillim* (praises) in Hebrew, the psalms played a central role in liturgical worship where they were sung to the accompaniment of music. Through the psalms, worshippers were invited to share the inner life of the psalmist and, by appropriating the experiences that occasioned them, they too were able to live their life as a dialogue with God.

The Psalter is the book of the poor who call themselves 'poor and needy' or 'weak' (*'ani we ebion*, 40:17; 70:5). These are self-designations of those who in the depth of their need come into the presence of the Lord to plead with him to intervene and save. They are the suffering, victims of injustice, persecuted, slandered, falsely accused and unable to defend themselves. They appeal to the Lord for mercy and help in obtaining justice (9:18; 10:12, 8–11). Most often they lacked social status, were underprivileged or dispossessed. They place their trust in the Lord, hoping to find comfort and support to reverse their fortunes. Other characteristics were: 'righteous' (*sadiq*, 37:12) in contrast to the wicked and ungodly who accuse the righteous unjustly; 'servants' (*'abadim*, 19:11, 13) of the Lord; and 'pious' (*hasidim*, 30:4), who are conscious of their commitment and loyalty to the Lord and live in obedience to his will.

Only those who actually lived the attitudes articulated in the psalms deserve to be called the true people of God. Those who prayed the psalms were full of hope and expectation. They 'waited' for the Lord (40:1) and were constantly on the lookout for his intervention. In the depths of their souls, the seat of all need and desire, they kept hope alive and active. This hope was not confined to the liturgy or the Temple, for their God was one who journeyed with his faithful ones. For this journey, God's law defined for them a path and a way that guided their steps in daily life: 'Your word is a lamp for my feet, a light on my path' (Ps 119:105). Their relationship to the law is characterised by love, joy and eagerness; it does not betray traits of a rigid religiosity or legalistic observance.

It was people such as those described in the psalms who in every generation became carriers of God's revelation, the true people of God. From the disciples of Isaiah to the poor of Zephaniah, from Jeremiah and the Suffering Servant to those anonymous people who prayed and lived the spirit of the psalms, these constituted the faithful remnant who opened their souls to God in faith and trust as they awaited the coming of the Saviour-Messiah.

Endnotes

1   Here I am indebted to Michael W. Duggan, *The Consuming Fire: A Christian Guide to the Old Testament*, Huntington, Indiana: Our Sunday Visitor, 2010, pp. 167–178.

2   *Ibid.*, pp. 262–294.

3   *Ibid.*, pp. 475–492.

CHAPTER TEN:
THE COMING OF CHRIST

Introduction

As well as the expectation of a Saviour-Messiah from the line of David, there was already in Deuteronomy (18:15–18) the promise of a new Moses: 'I will raise up a prophet like yourself for them from their own brothers. I will put my words into his mouth and he shall tell them all I command him' (v. 18). For during the course of Israelite history, it had become obvious that taking possession of the promised land did not constitute the Israelites' entry into the fulfilment for which they longed. They were still waiting for a real liberation from a new Moses-like figure who would show them the true face of God and the path to reach him. This promise of a prophet like Moses was fulfilled and surpassed in Jesus who said: 'To have seen me is to have seen the Father' (Jn 14:9). Jesus didn't bring world peace, universal prosperity or a better world. What he brought was the true God.

> He has brought the God who formerly unveiled his countenance gradually, first to Abraham, then to Moses and the prophets, and then in the wisdom literature – the God who revealed his face only in Israel, even though he was also honoured among the pagans in various shadowy guises. It is this God, the God of Abraham, Isaac and Jacob, the true God, whom he brought to the nations of the earth.[1]

Jesus brought not only the true God, but also the definitive truth about our origin and destiny. In Jesus, God's power works quietly in our world. It is a force that endures and saves. Its core content is the kingdom of God, which is not a territory but a person. Through his miracles and teaching in parables, Jesus reveals not an abstract God, but a God who cares, acts and intervenes in our lives. Jesus leads people to realise that, in him, God is present among them in a new way.

> The symbolism of the incarnation would express the experience, with a date in history, of God reaching into man and revealing him as the Presence that is the flow of presence from the beginning of the world to its end. History is Christ written large.[2]

Jesus proclaimed a living God who acts concretely in the world and in history. From the very beginning, Israel was to become the bearer of a universal promise (Gn 12:1–3) and the vehicle for this universalisation has now become the new community founded by Jesus that we call Church.

> Through Jesus' presence and action, God has here and now entered actively into history in a wholly new way. The reason why *now* is the fulness of time (Mk 1:15), why *now* is in a unique sense the time of conversion and penance, as well as a time of joy, is that in Jesus it is God who draws near to us. In Jesus, God is now the one who acts and who rules as Lord – rules in a divine way, without worldly power, rules through love that reaches 'to the end' (Jn 13:1) to the Cross.[3]

Christians believe that Jesus provides the full truth regarding the human condition as we experience it. He reveals the true God as a loving Father, whose pull or drawing has now become effective concretely through Jesus by making God accessible to us in person. Christians also believe that Jesus is the answer to the human search, the sense of wonder and questioning that has always troubled human beings. Guided by Church teaching, they have a clearer understanding of the source of reality – God's love (Jn 3:16–17) – and the goal of reality – a future that entails the complete transformation of human beings (Jn 11:25; 1 Cor 15:20–58). The Christian life, then, becomes a joyful pilgrimage to our destination, an open existence in a faith that works through charity and is lived in hope. It is a process of transformation taking place even now to prepare us to share in God's life for all eternity.

We have access to the life, death and resurrection of Jesus through the four gospels that narrate the story of the unknown God now fully revealed in Jesus Christ; in his words (inaugurating the kingdom of God), in his deeds of power (healings and exorcisms) and through his death and resurrection.[4] The story of Jesus, then, is both informative and performative, i.e. it has the ability to change people. It was first promulgated by those who had experienced Jesus during his earthly ministry, who accepted and understood his message, articulated it first in preaching and teaching, and subsequently expressed it in written language. The events of Jesus' life were remembered, recalled in the liturgy, in preaching, teaching, missionary outreach and in controversies with opponents. Disciples gained a deeper appreciation of who Jesus was and of his mission as they continued to live a Christian life in the Spirit. These experiences were later written down in the four gospels in the form of history-like stories, or story-like histories, with the result that the truth about Jesus and his mission became much clearer – revealing God's ways with human beings and the truth of the human condition, resulting in an entirely new way of living.

There is the temptation nowadays to reduce Jesus Christ, the Son of God, to a historical person, a mere man, comprehensible within the parameters of historiography as presently practised. But this 'historical' Jesus is more likely to be an image of the authors' desires and longings than of the living God who came to dwell among us. For the real historical Jesus cannot be adequately grasped independently of the faith of the first witnesses and those who subsequently handed on the story. Nevertheless, if it is true that God became a human being and entered history, then the quest for historical knowledge is fully justified. Jesus, the Jew, brought the hopes and longings of Israel to fulfilment. The gospels, however, which recount the life of Jesus, found their setting within the liturgy. It was there that the word of God was proclaimed as Good News and where the profound truth about the mystery of Jesus and his mission were unveiled in greater depth. The people of Israel, together with their scriptures, provided a *context* for the life and mission of Jesus that helped elucidate the purpose of his mission and reveal the mystery of his person.

The first accounts of what Jesus had done were fashioned with help from Israel's traditions and were shaped by the early Christian community, but they cannot be grasped without faith. Faith and trust also have to do with knowledge, the result of a personal encounter rather than an analysis of what Jesus said and did. Here affection, love and loyalty, fidelity and devotion yield a different kind of knowledge, for the language of objective facts is limited. The evangelists' portrait of Jesus that we find in the gospels is the only real, historical Jesus. That is why a combination of study and encounter on the part of the believer gives a more rounded and accurate picture of who Jesus was. The promised future adumbrated in the Old Testament is beginning now through the person and mission of Jesus. The reign of God is 'already' present, the 'not yet' aspect of this reign is in the future and so we pray 'thy kingdom come' to hasten its fulfilment.

Jesus used images and metaphors to clarify aspects of the reign of God which was already becoming a reality. Some forty parables describe various aspects of that reign with illustrations taken from everyday experience in order to explode customary pious ways of thinking. By means of these, Jesus instructed, taught, corrected, warned and preached the reign of God. Along with parables, Jesus performed deeds of power (miracles) and signs that were an integral part of his ministry. Through his healings and exorcisms, Jesus confronted the powers of evil and chaos and healed a damaged and distorted world so that the reign of God could become visible and tangible in the present. But miracles occur only where faith is present. With the coming of Jesus, then, we have the saving story that provides answers to the questions of life and death: 'This is eternal life, that they should know you the only true God and the one whom you sent, Jesus Christ' (Jn 17:3).

What may be called 'open existence' is the recognition of creatureliness and finitude, the acceptance of the human condition as experienced together with its restlessness *and* acceptance through grace of the invitation to follow Jesus as the way, the truth and the life. The Gospel of John captures the drawing power of the risen Christ and identifies it with the pull exerted by the unknown God: 'No one can come to me unless he is drawn by the Father who sent me, and I will raise him up at the last day' (6:44); 'When I am lifted up from the earth, I shall draw all men to myself' (12:32).

Saint Paul elaborates the directional movement of history to its goal beyond death in 1 Corinthians 15 and gives directives to resolve concrete problems in Christian living in the 'in-between', which become emblematic of the type of problems and their resolution that Christians encounter in every age.

What is a Gospel?[25]

The gospels tell the story of Jesus Christ in narrative form as the preferred means to communicate the mystery of his person and mission, and their implications for discipleship. They present the origins of the Good News in the life and ministry of Jesus who first embodied it in his own person, and they endeavour to link the identity between Jesus of Nazareth and the risen Christ who is now alive and active in the heart of the Christian community. Jesus is presented as someone whose earthly life and glorified presence are still relevant to readers today. In addition, the four gospels function to shape the identity of the readers. Their purpose is not only to inform, but also to transform the lives of readers by involving them in the story of Jesus and calling them to become his disciples. Each of the gospels tells its story within a broad biographical framework as a literary means of relating the remembered and interpreted story of Jesus in the light of the resurrection and the coming of the Spirit. The experiences, insights and problems of the early Christian communities also played a not insignificant part in the actual telling of the story against the Old Testament background that helped in the task of interpretation and elucidation.

Each gospel is a literary and theological whole. As stories, they are meant to engage the reader personally. They are historical insofar as they tell of a historical person. At a deeper level, though, they are stories that history cannot fully assess, for example Jesus' incarnation, his resurrection and glorification. These lie beyond the historian's competence, and yet they form the most important part of the story that conveys the meaning and significance of the Christ event. The gospel narratives take on a life of their own as literary works independent of their authors and intended readers. As an integral part of the canon of scripture established by the Church, they are best understood within that community.

Contemporary readers need a basic self-awareness and a reflective attitude as they approach the gospels. At the experiential centre of Christianity is God's love for us human beings:

> God's love for us was revealed when God sent into the world his only Son so that we could have life through him; this is the love I mean: not our love for God, but God's love for us when he sent his Son to be the sacrifice that takes our sins away. (1 Jn 4:9–10)

The response to that love is faith and conversion, a grace that is also an insight that the promises made by God in Jesus Christ concern each reader *personally*. With this realisation, readers pass from a notional or theoretical to a real assent, and can be said to be undergoing a conversion experience. The story told in the gospels becomes their story when they allow themselves to be transformed as a result. For outward and visible membership of the Church is by itself no guarantee that a person has been converted. Members of the Christian community benefit from the story of Jesus only to the extent that they allow themselves to be shaped by it. When they do, Jesus' message then becomes *evangelium* (Good News), not because it is immediately pleasing or attractive, but because it comes from him who provides the key to true happiness. Truth is not always comfortable for human beings, yet it is only truth that makes us free and only freedom that brings us joy.

Mark

The Gospel of Mark is centred on the person of Christ, on his activity more than on his teaching. The God revealed in Mark is one who acts with power in Jesus Christ to heal all kinds of human brokenness, examples and summaries of which are found in the first half of his Gospel (1:1–8:30). In the second half, the passion story gradually comes to dominate. Jesus reveals a new and strange God, while his passion points to a particular understanding of God's reconciling love: 'For the Son of Man himself did not come to be served, but to serve and to give his life as a ransom for many' (10:45). Jesus, in his manner of living and dying, reveals the authentic face of the true God. Two lengthy chapters (14:1–15:47) reveal how important the passion is for Mark. Jesus' death on behalf of others sums up his entire mission and the ultimate revelation of his identity as Son of God. The crucifixion, death and burial bring the great drama to its conclusion when the pagan centurion confesses Jesus as the Son of God (15:39). A final episode proclaims that the crucified Jesus is victorious over death (16:1–8).

Mark has succeeded in presenting a moving narrative about Jesus that traces his ministry from his baptism at the Jordan river through his preaching tour in Galilee, his journey to Jerusalem and his death and resurrection. Because the message of Jesus called for a radical change in lifestyle on the part of his listeners and challenged the reigning powers, it is hardly surprising that conflict and suffering have such a prominent place in the narrative. The passion story at the end dominates the whole when Jesus is arrested, condemned and executed. Despite gaps and inconsistencies, the Gospel of Mark presents a coherent narrative capable of having a powerful effect on readers when they allow themselves to be caught up in the drama of the story. A new way of looking at the world around them is opened up.

Jesus carried out his mission, Mark informs us, not only by what he said and did, but most of all by what was done to him and by what he suffered. Nevertheless, it is not his sufferings as such that save us, it is the *love* with which he embraced them. He willingly and freely offered his life out of love for human beings (10:45). The way of the cross, the pattern of Jesus' self-transcendent love, is, according to Mark, the only way to authentic human existence. He invites us to take up our cross and follow in his footsteps:

> If anyone wishes to be a follower of mine, let him renounce himself and take up his cross and follow me. For anyone who wants to save his life will lose it; but anyone who loses his life for my sake, and for the sake of the gospel, will find it (8:34–35).

In our own experience too, our lives are also determined more by what is done to us than by what we do ourselves. As we journey through life, things happen to us that are completely outside of our control. For example, illness, suffering and anguish; failure, disappointment and tragedy; loss of friends, breakdown in relationships and the death of those nearest to us. As we grow older, there is the onset of old age, with its accompanying limitations, and eventually death. All of these are part of what it means to be human, and nobody escapes them. The value of suffering, however, lies not in the pain of it, but in what we choose to make of it. Though the road of suffering is never an easy one, it is not the same since Jesus traversed it. Since the risen Lord is someone who suffered and died, suffering and death are overcome, though not eliminated. Although this answer may not fully satisfy rational human beings, it is a consolation to know that Jesus has gone down the road of suffering ahead of us and can accompany us in our suffering as well. In turning to Jesus in our suffering, we encounter a God who knows first-hand the pain and sorrow of living in a fallen world, one who knows and understands (Heb 4:15). God suffers with us. Mark assures us that if we unite our suffering with that of Jesus, we too will share in his victory over suffering and death and in his Easter glory.

Matthew

The Gospel of Matthew presupposes the initial preaching of the Good News, faith, conversion and baptism into the community of Jesus' disciples, and the experience of new life in Christ. The gift of God precedes the demand of God – how the baptised are to live out their Christian life in community living. For authentic commitment to the gift of God's love given to us in Jesus is possible only within the community where the risen Lord continues to be present (28:20). It is here that disciples mature in their foundational experience of God's love in the company of those who have freely submitted to his rule in Jesus Christ. That is why Matthew gives considerable teaching on discipleship, not only in the five lengthy sermons that characterise his work, but throughout the narrative sections as well. Adherence to Jesus is gauged by fidelity to the demands of fraternal love, first of all, within the community itself.

Matthew equips the newly baptised with guidelines and concrete directives for fostering such a love and serves as a practical initiation into the life of the Christian community. The baptised who have now become disciples have taken upon themselves the yoke of Jesus to learn from him (11:29) and the Church becomes the discipleship of Jesus' family (12:49–50). Matthew regards the Christian community made up of Jews and Gentiles as the continuation of the Old Testament people of God. He achieves this by his frequent use of Old Testament fulfilment quotations. The true Israel is now to be found in the Christian community founded by Jesus on Peter (16:13–20) and led by the apostles, who are invested with Christ's own authority (28:16–20).

The Sermon on the Mount (chs. 5–7) paints a comprehensive portrait of Christian living. The content of this teaching is not a law code but a collection of principles, precepts and exhortations that describe the life and behaviour of disciples. It provides paradigms or models of attitudes, character and actions to shape the identity and lifestyle of disciples within the Christian community – what they are to become (the beatitudes) and how they are to behave, guided by the principle of love (7:12).

> If being human is essentially about relation to God, it is clear that speaking with, and listening to, God is an essential part of it. That is why the Sermon on the Mount also includes a teaching on prayer.[6]

The Church, however, is not some kind of exclusive, cosy club of like-minded individuals that becomes an end in itself. Throughout the gospel, Jesus is both teacher and guide who models what disciples are to become as a community in order to go out and evangelise the world.

Luke-Acts

Luke-Acts is a two-volume work which serves the needs of Christians who are already committed to Jesus Christ and living out that commitment in the community he formed to reach out to the outside world. Disciples need to be intellectually equipped to confront the social, political, economic, cultural and religious complexities of life outside the Christian community to which they are sent. The situation towards the end of the first century called for a new synthesis of the traditions in a powerful, well-articulated literary narrative, and this two-volume work is intended to be read as such. Luke provides an account of Jesus' life and teaching followed by a narrative of the disciples' missionary work and preaching (Acts), to equip readers for a universal mission in the world. He wants to show that the gospel message is not limited to any one culture, for the story of Jesus belongs to all people.

The evangelist's original contribution was to connect events in the early Church to those of Jesus' ministry and to the whole story of God's people in the Old Testament (Lk 1–2; Acts 1:1–5). Luke describes Jesus as emerging from within the best in Judaism, the 'anawim, the poor who prayerfully awaited the fulfilment of God's promises made to their ancestors. The joyful expectation of Israel's long-awaited Messiah has become a reality in the birth of Jesus. Through him God's peace and blessings will reach both Jew and Gentile (2:29–32). This worldwide mission is carried out in Acts (1:8) under the guidance of the Spirit. There is continuity in God's plan of salvation from beginning to end.

Luke's portrait of Jesus is characterised by qualities of mercy, compassion, love, charm, delicacy and joy, a prophet with great concern for others. Dante has described Luke as 'the scribe of the gentleness of Christ'. Some of the more memorable stories of divine compassion are found only in Luke: the widow of Naim (7:11–17), the prodigal son (15:11–32), Zacchaeus (19:1–10). His ministry is a source of joy which permeates the entire gospel. In Luke, Jesus is the Saviour sent to seek out and save the lost. His mission is carried out in a spirit of prayer.

Christians, according to Luke, are those living in continuity with the disciples whose story fills Luke-Acts and who later became known as Christians (Acts 11:26). The call of Peter is emblematic of the call of disciples (Lk 5:1–11). *Disciples* are identified by their relationship to Jesus, the Teacher; they are taught by him and listen to him. Their lives are patterned on Jesus' teaching and they become an identifiable group who acknowledge Jesus as Lord. They are willing to become *followers* of Jesus, which involves leaving everything behind (Lk 5:11) and this following is inseparable from taking up one's cross 'every day' (Lk 9:23). To follow Jesus means to accompany him through suffering to glory (Lk 24:26). This solidarity is a response to Jesus who gave his own life, transcended death and will later accompany them on mission through the Spirit. Disciples who become followers are also *forerunners* (Lk 10:1) who prepare the way for the Lord's return in glory by going on mission to the ends of the earth. The role of forerunners may be compared to that of John the Baptist who prepared for Jesus' coming in history.

Acts continues the story begun by Luke in his gospel. The Good News must be spread to all peoples of the world (Lk 24:47;

Acts 1:8). He has made use of inherited traditions and the art of storytelling to narrate the development of God's plan of salvation in the apostolic age (AD 30–62) but does not provide a detailed chronicle of the Church's missionary outreach. Luke models his account on Old Testament historiography to show how God's plan of salvation worked out through special people and events. God intervenes through the Spirit at critical turning points in the story. The evangelist adds speeches that announce the Good News as well as miracles worked by the apostles in Jesus' name. All of this takes place amid persecutions, trials, imprisonments and dramatic shipwrecks as he describes the development of the early Church.

It is the Spirit who enables and transforms the apostles to continue the outreach of Jesus to all kinds of people – powerful and weak, wealthy and poor, men and women, poor widows and provincial governors, kings and philosophers as well as Jews. For Luke, the end of the story of Jesus is his Church. Jesus' ministry is the beginning of the continuing history of the Church as it reaches out to the whole world, symbolised by Paul's arrival in Rome, the capital of the empire. Christian churches now dot the empire. Henceforth, the story of salvation will involve all peoples of the world. Acts represents the breakthrough of Christianity to universality as a world religion.

John

The Gospel of John contains a more developed Christology (1:1–18), and shows the universal relevance of Jesus for both Jew and pagan alike: 'the Saviour of the world' (4:42). It is the story in language of what was experienced, understood, meditated on, articulated and expressed in the historical events in the life of Jesus. The disciples believed that God spoke and acted through these events. What was important for this evangelist was the revelation of the true God and how people responded to it. This insight is now transmitted with a deeper understanding and written down in story-like fashion. By accepting this story and responding to it, one becomes a Christian, a member of God's family (1:12).

The Gospel of John begins with an overview of the central character, Jesus, as the pre-existent Word, and ends with Jesus as the exalted Son of God. The gospel presents Jesus 'from above' by identifying him with the Word, through whom God created the universe. Jesus is equal to God, makes God known, exercises functions attributed to God (giving life and judging, 5:19–47) and appropriates the divine name 'I am' revealed to Moses (8:28, 58). Humans ought to respond to Jesus with the honour appropriate to God. Now risen, he sends his Spirit to encourage, inspire and instruct his disciples (16:7–11). The result is that the full reality and significance of Jesus, the revealer of the true God, is disclosed.

The development of John's story is propelled by conflict between belief and unbelief as responses to Jesus' revelation. In the first half of the gospel, Jesus confronts a variety of people in everyday situations (e.g. Nicodemus, the Samaritan woman, the royal official, the paralytic, the blind man, opponents, disciples, etc). The reader can identify with them in their various responses to Jesus. All are confronted with deciding for or against Jesus. The positive and negative responses as well as misunderstandings are typical, and readers are also obliged to choose, to allow themselves to be drawn to the Father through Jesus.

At the Last Supper, Jesus delivers lengthy discourses to his disciples about the love that should characterise his followers. He prepares them for the paschal events as well as for their future life as a community of believers. The evangelist understands the crucifixion of Jesus as the moment of his life-giving exaltation and return to the Father.

In the allegory of the vine and the branches, its exposition and application (15:1–17), Jesus co-opts symbols and ideas that were part of the religious heritage of Israel. Jesus is the genuine vine and Christians are called to have an intimate, living relationship with him like branches of the vine. If they are to be at rights with God, they must 'abide in' (*menein en*) him. Their contact with Christ makes them fruitful branches and shows them to be disciples of Jesus. Bearing fruit connotes the works of love required of Jesus' followers within the faith community. It becomes the tangible sign of discipleship, a visual image of the life of the Christian community that is shaped by love and grounded in Jesus' presence. For the fruitfulness of each branch depends on its relationship to the vine, one that is measured by the community's fruits – to love as Jesus loved:

> I give you a new commandment: love one another as I have loved
> you, you also must love one another. By this love that you have
> for one another, everyone will know that you are my disciples.
> (13:34–35)

The distinctiveness of the Christian community derives solely
from its relationship to God and Jesus. Jesus' invitation to 'abide'
(used ten times in 15:1–10) means steadfastness and perseverance
in communion with the Lord amid the ups and downs of life and
includes prayer as an essential element (v. 7).

The Gospel's articulation of human existence as modelled by
Jesus sets a standard for human beings by developing a vocabulary
of personal and interpersonal relationships based on the triune God:
'The Father and I are one' (10:30). Jesus offers *agape* as mutual and
unconditional love exemplified by Jesus: 'Love one another just as I
have loved you' (13:34), a love based on the relationship of Father
and Son (15:9–15), even to the extent of laying down one's life
for another (15:13). Jesus revealed a new depth in inter-personal
relationships – unconditional love as the norm of human life that
is mutual, unconditional, personal and interpersonal, that leads
to unity with God and one another: 'that they may be one in us'
(17:21). The essence of humanity is therefore friendship with God:

> You are my friends if you do what I command you … I call you
> friends because I have made known to you everything I have learnt
> from my Father. (Jn 15:14, 15)

Christ brought with him a new experience of humanity that was
later articulated by John (and Paul) and in time became the spiritual
foundation of Western civilisation because of its universality.

Conclusion

Prospective believers who wish to follow Jesus have the gospels to
guide them through the essential stages of Christian maturity. The
four gospels fulfil the need to experience and explain in-depth,
both to oneself and to others, what the Christian faith is all about
and how it is solidly founded on Jesus Christ as the way and the
truth to an authentic human life. The four gospels articulate the

essential dimensions of the Christian life: Christological (centred on relationship with Christ – Mark); ecclesial (lived out in the Christian community – Matthew); missionary (for the sake of the world – Luke-Acts); and contemplative ('abiding in' Christ through faith, love and hope – John). In this way, believers are equipped to explain their hopes, convictions and lifestyle to those who ask:

> Always have your answer ready for people who ask you for the reason for the hope that you all have. But give it with courtesy and respect and with a clear conscience. (1 Pt 3:15–16)

Christian belief offers truth as a lifestyle, not as a mere perception or idea, for only by becoming a way of life does it become *our* truth and makes a claim on us. Christianity regards human beings as capable of recognising the truth that stands before them in the person of Jesus Christ. For Jesus is not merely a manifestation of the divine, but *is* God. In him, God has shown his human face. If in Christ, this new gift of truth is being granted to us, then it is our duty and privilege to offer it to others freely.

Endnotes

1   Joseph Ratzinger, *Jesus of Nazareth: From the Baptism in the Jordan to the Transfiguration*, New York: Doubleday, 2007, p. 44.

2   Eric Voegelin, 'Immortality: Experience and Symbol,' in *Published Essays 1966– 1985 (The Collected Works of Eric Voegelin, vol. 12)*, (E. Sandoz, ed.), Baton Rouge: LSUP, 1990, p. 78.

3   Ratzinger, *Jesus of Nazareth*, pp. 60–61.

4   Raymond E. Brown, *An Introduction to the New Testament*, New York: Doubleday, 1997, pp. 1–96.

5   *Ibid.*, pp. 99–382. For further reading, see Rudolf Schnackenburg, *Jesus in the Gospels: A Biblical Christology*, Louisville, KY: Westminster, John Knox Press, 1995. See also, Maurice Hogan, *The Four Gospels: Following in the Footsteps of Jesus*, Dublin: Veritas, 2015. For a more extended treatment, see Michael Mullins' commentaries on the four gospels and Acts of the Apostles, Dublin: Columba Press, 2003–2013.

6   Ratzinger, *Jesus of Nazareth*, p. 128.

CHAPTER ELEVEN:
ASSIMILATION OF THE CHRIST-EVENT

Significance of the Christ-Event

We come to know Jesus Christ through the gospels when we internalise the *experiences* articulated therein, as we have seen above. We must now make the connection between Jesus and the questions people ask about the mystery of life and human beings, their origin, destiny and life in the world. Saint Paul articulates in depth the meaning of the Christ-event and its implications for daily living in his correspondence.[1]

Paul concentrates on the paschal events – Christ suffered and died for sinful humanity by offering himself as a sacrifice out of love; his resurrection is the beginning of the resurrection of all believers (Phil 3:21). The apostle emphasises the effects of the passion, death and resurrection of Jesus Christ that for him are the climactic events of Jesus' ministry and alludes to only a few events in Jesus' public life. In his personal presentation of the Christ-event, the content that he preached is summed up in the cross: 'We preach a crucified Christ; to the Jews an obstacle they cannot get over, to the pagans madness, but to those who have been called … a Christ who is the power and the wisdom of God' (1 Cor 1:24–25). The cross symbolised for Paul the self-sacrificial love of Christ for each one of us: 'I live in faith: faith in the Son of God who loved *me* and who sacrificed himself for my sake' (Gal 2:20, emphasis added). The 'story of the cross' is the power of God unleased in the world for the salvation of all: 'Jesus who was put to death for our sins and raised to life to justify us' (Rm 4:25). Thus, the gospel comes not in words alone but with the power of the Spirit 'for everyone who has faith' (Rm 1:16). This interior commitment to Christ, although not outwardly visible, must gradually pervade Christians' conscious life and behaviour.

Paul uses various images to express distinctive aspects of the mystery of Christ in its *effects*. These vivid metaphors are taken from the religious and social life of his time: *justification* – the broken relationship between God and human beings due to sin has been gratuitously put right by the death of Christ (Rm 5:19); *salvation* – Christians have been rescued from evil and death (Col 1:13); *reconciliation* – Christians have been restored from enmity to friendship with God (Rm 5:10–11); *expiation* – Christ's sacrifice on the cross is the means by which our sins are blotted out (Rm 3:25); *redemption* – Christians are released from slavery to sin and death (Rm 8:23); *freedom* – Christians, even now, enjoy a new social status as citizens of heaven (Phil 3:20); *sanctification* – Christians are dedicated to God and oriented to serving him (Rm 12:1–2); *transformation* – Christians undergo a reshaping to fit them for participation in the divine life (Phil 3:21); *new creation* – Christians already share in the risen life of Christ through baptism (Gal 2:20); and *glorification* – Christians will share in the glory Christ now enjoys (Rm 8:30).

From the Old Testament, Paul was heir to a rich heritage regarding the situation of humanity before the coming of Christ and the reality we call sin. Beginning with the narrative of Adam and Eve, sin manifested itself essentially as disobedience by violating God's prohibition (Gn 2:17). But prior to this was an interior act, namely, at the suggestion of the devil, the couple wished to decide for themselves between good and evil, claiming thereby sole mastery over their destiny (Gn 3:1–7). The mystery of sin therefore goes beyond the human world. The Book of Wisdom (2:24) identifies the serpent with the devil or Satan who reappears in the gospels.

It is not surprising, then, that this radical perversion entailed grave consequences for the couple. Expelled from paradise and the tree of life, only death awaited them. In the meantime, sin proliferated (Gn 4–11) and put its mark on the subsequent history of the chosen people. The lesson from this is of primary importance: humans who think they can live independently of God usually do so at others' expense (2 Sm 12) and it has negative effects on the human heart as well. By transgressing God's precepts given for our flourishing, humans end by destroying themselves. Sin is a refusal to be loved by God, but God does not cease to offer his love. However, to remedy the situation is beyond the power of human beings. They need a new heart and a new spirit (Ez 36:26ff). This interior transformation will be accomplished by the self-offering of the Suffering Servant (Is 53) whose identity for the moment remains mysterious.

The New Testament reveals the identity of this servant as none other than the Son of God become man, who came to bring the full revelation of the love of God and the true nature of sin. Paul develops a theology of sin and, in the Letter to the Romans, lists specific sins which are the expression and exteriorisation of a hostility towards God and his kingdom preached and embodied by Jesus Christ. He reviews the situation of humanity apart from Christ as one of alienation from God resulting in moral and social ills (Rm 1:18–32). All human beings, Paul asserts, both pagan and Jew (2:1–3:20), are guilty, under sin's dominion (3:9) and in bondage to Satan. Yet they still desire to do good but are incapable of accomplishing it (7:16, 22) and are unable to avoid the consequences – eternal death (v. 24). Paul stresses the universality and tyranny of sin to show human powerlessness and to reveal the necessity of Jesus' liberating work. Human nature is flawed, damaged and wounded and in need of healing and restoration. We cannot heal ourselves, we need a Saviour (v. 25). The apostle recalls the solidarity of the entire human race with Adam only to reveal a superior solidarity with Christ (5:12–21). 'God has included all men in disobedience only that he might show himself merciful to all' (11:32) and this evokes a response of grateful admiration (v. 33).

The victory over sin and Satan is the result of the mission of Jesus. The gospels present his public life as a struggle against the power of Satan that is evident in his deliverance of the possessed. This battle reached its climax at the passion. The resurrection of Jesus marks the defeat of Satan, but the struggle will only be concluded at the end of time (1 Cor 15:24–28). In the meantime, the Christian must choose between God and Satan: 'For it is not against human enemies that we have to struggle, but against the Sovereignties and the Powers who originate the darkness of this world, the spiritual army of evil in the heavens' (Eph 6:12). During our time on earth we are saved through hope (Rm 8:24); ours is a heritage that will be fully manifest only at the end of time. We await the final manifestation of the Saviour who will complete his work of transforming our bodies to be like his own in glory (Phil 3:20–21).

In the resurrection of Christ, what is affirmed is that God himself and the communion he offers are true life for human beings. To belong to him is to be rooted in indestructible life. Baptism grafts us into the death of Christ (Rm 6:4) which is ordered to resurrection. Accordingly, suffering and dying with Christ brings with them the hope of resurrection. The future life is ordered to a transformation of all life, both for human beings and the world at large. Paul affirms and attempts to explain the real bodily resurrection of those in Christ. He begins with the fact of Christ's resurrection (1 Cor 15:1–11) and that the resurrection of Christians is an equal certainty (vv. 12–19). Christ is the first fruits (*aparche*, v. 20) of those who have died, the first of a harvest that is sure to follow. With the risen Christ, hope takes a new form, because death no longer has the last word (vv. 54–58).

> The risen Lord is rightly called 'first fruits of those who have fallen asleep,' not merely because he has initiated the universal resurrection of the just, but also because his own glorified humanity will one day effectively realise in us the final object of Christian faith and hope.[2]

Having affirmed the fact of Christ's resurrection and the certainty of the resurrection of those united to him, Paul attempts to explain how a marvellous transformation takes place by using the analogy of a grain of seed. The grain that is sown is not what it is to become, yet there is identity between the risen stalk and the buried grain. The resurrection body is not only of the same species, it is the same individual body, although transformed. Paul uses a series of contrasts to explain this transfiguration: human beings will be changed from corruption to incorruption, from dishonour to glory, from weakness to power, from natural to spiritual, from perishable to imperishable (vv. 42–44). With 15:45 begins a whole series of lyrical parallels emphasising the superiority of the last Adam (Christ) over the first with regard to the kind of existence each communicates to human beings, for 'flesh and blood cannot inherit the kingdom of God: and the perishable cannot inherit what lasts forever' (15:50). The human nature which we have all inherited from Adam is powerless in itself to attain to the fulness of divine life which communion with God entails and so we must be empowered to transcend our earthly limitations.

The risen Christ is the new Adam of a new humanity endowed with creative power which the first Adam did not possess. The life in the body which we now possess is to be transformed into a spiritual and glorious body (*soma pneumatikon*, v.44). This process, already begun in baptism, will be completed at the *parousia*. For Paul, death is not an escape of the soul from the prison of the body, but the beginning of a transformation of the whole physical person into a spiritual one.

> Paul steered a remarkably consistent course between, on the one hand, a materialistic doctrine of physical resurrection and, on the other hand, a dualistic doctrine of the escape of the soul from the body; and that the secret of his consistency here is his tenacious grasp of the central theme: Jesus, Son of God.[3]

In his body of glory, Christ is the true human being, and the Christian will one day realise a similar stature. Paul's Adamic Christology functions to give assurance to the believer as to what kind of future existence is to be his and how it is to be obtained. It is Christ, not Adam, who is the authentic human being who assures us of our eschatological humanity. True human fulfilment is not to be found in looking back to the old creation, but in looking forward to the new one already fulfilled in Christ who will also 'transform our lowly body that it may be conformed to the body of his glory' (Phil 3:21). The nature of Christ's resurrected existence is a human nature as well as divine (*anthropos*, 1 Cor 15:21, 47); even in his exalted state he is still a human being and so Christ and the believer are intimately related in their essential humanity. At one and the same time, Christ is the visible image (*eikon*, Col 1:15) of the unseen God and the embodiment of the true humanity willed by God at creation (Gn 1:26–28).

Elsewhere in his writings, Paul is aware that in explaining the grandeur of the Christian life and its destiny, he is attempting to describe the indescribable: 'We teach what scripture calls: "the things that no eye has seen and no ear has heard, things beyond the mind of man, all that God has prepared for those who love him"' (1

Cor 2:9). He realises that it is impossible to describe fully how the encounter with God will take place. We can only speak about future spiritual realities in images taken from human experience when we talk about God and life with him. What we say about them is more different from the reality than similar to it. All statements about God and the afterlife are, therefore, *analogous*, that is, the dissimilarity to images and concepts in our everyday experience is unimaginably greater than the similarities.

Since the human spirit is one with the body, it is their unity that makes a human being a person. Both body and soul are realities only as oriented to each other. They constitute a single human being though they are not identical. The body is wholly defined by reference to the soul, which develops a living body as its corporeal expression. That is why the soul cannot leave behind its relationship with the body and why theology speaks of the resurrection of the body rather than the immortality of the soul. The body is the vitality of the soul because the soul is the actuality of the body that makes a person open to immortality. Human beings are defined by their relationship with God because they are capable of knowledge and love of God. The human capacity for truth and love is where eternal life can break forth.

With Paul's insistence on the resurrection of the body, we have rediscovered the indivisibility of the human being. Immortality is promised not to a separated soul but to the whole person who goes on existing in a transformed state. Christ in glory is the authentic human being and model of what Christians are to become. There will be a transformation of *persons* who will possess a new quality that is imperishable, immortal and glorious, and yet identical with their past. This will be complete when all humanity and the world itself is renewed. Resurrection on the 'last day' would then indicate the biblical, communal character of human immortality, which is related to the whole of humanity and to the whole of the universe. The essential content of the Pauline symbolisation is that human beings live on, not by virtue of their own power, but because they are known and loved by God in such a manner that they cannot perish. And since human and cosmic relationships are also part of what it is to be human, the individual will only be complete when the whole of humanity and the cosmos are brought to fulfilment. This is the Christian response to the enigma of death; for without an intelligible answer to the question of death, no light can be thrown on the question of human life and purpose.

In Christ alone, therefore, the complete answer about what human beings are and will become is disclosed. They are not yet fully themselves; rather, they are persons *en route* to becoming themselves in Christ. They are oriented towards the future when they will really appear complete as children of God:

> We are already the children of God, but what we are to be in the future has not yet been revealed; all we know is, that when it is revealed, we shall be like him because we shall see him as he really is. (1 Jn 3:2)

Relationship with God is what basically constitutes the human person; Christ is not only an example to be followed, but one who leads us to God and who alone can save us.

> Christian theology, if it is to be true to its origin, must be first and foremost a theology of the resurrection ... Its first and primordial statement is the good tidings that the power of death, the one constant of history, has, in a single instance, been broken by the power of God and that history has been imbued with an entirely new hope.[4]

Living in the In-Between

Hidden from view for the most part in Paul's theology are his ideas on what it means to be human. He presupposes certain things about human beings that were well-known to his recipients when he wrote as a missionary, pastoral theologian. Paul's anthropology was influenced by Jewish categories which he inherited – human beings as whole persons existing in different dimensions rather than made up of distinct parts of body and soul as in Greek thought. Human beings are essentially relational beings, and so his concern is with humankind and with each individual in their relationships to God, to one another as social beings, to God's creation and to Christ as God's response to the human predicament. Persons are defined by their relationships. What is important is how Paul uses the inherited terminology to which he adds some of his own.

Flesh (*basar, sarx*) – human beings are flesh in the sense that they are weak, contingent beings who belong to this world. As such they are vulnerable and exposed to the enticements of sin, to what is transient and perishable, to satisfy their merely human appetites and needs. They are unable by themselves to keep God's law. **Soul** (*nefesh, psyche*) – the soul denotes the person as conscious, living and full of vitality, filled with desires and longings, seeking and yearning, and aspiring to a fuller life. **Heart** (*lev, kardia*) – the innermost part of the person, the seat of thought, planning, reflection, decision and feeling; 'the experiencing, motivating I'. God alone can penetrate the heart. Renewal of the person involves a pure heart where one encounters God. **Spirit** (*ruach, pneuma*) – God's life-giving power that makes a person alive. It is the dimension of the person that relates most directly to God, the God-ward dimension. It reminds us that there is a greater depth or higher reality when the human spirit (psyche) opens up to the Spirit. Only then can the human spirit be whole. It needs God's protection and guidance, which is brought about by the Spirit of God. **Body** (*soma*) – not just the physical body but the whole person, by means of which a person relates to the environment as a personal embodied 'I'. It enables one to interact with the environment and cooperate with others, as well as emphasising the social dimension of bodiliness, of being in the world. In the resurrection of the body, Paul envisages the transformation of persons in their embodiment that will be appropriate to the spiritual world beyond death. **Flesh and blood** (*sarx kai haima*) – the human being in its frailty. **Mind** (*nous*) – the knowing and judging subject with a capacity for understanding, planning and decision. Humans can perceive the existence and nature of God rationally. Endowed with reason they can worship God and make ethical decisions; 'the thinking I'. **Conscience** (*syneidesis*) – consciousness of the moral aspects of one's actions and the capacity to judge one's actions. **Life** (*zoe*) – human existence as God's gift, the concrete human being, the subject of one's actions.

Paul's conception of the human person is that of a being who functions within several dimensions. As embodied beings, humans are social and can enter into relationships as a vital dimension of their existence. Our being of flesh attests to human frailty or weakness and so vulnerable to manipulation by our appetites and desires. At the same time, humans are also rational beings who can reflect and understand. As experiencing beings, they are capable of emotion and sustained motivation. As living beings, they are animated by the mystery of life as a gift from God. Lastly, there is a dimension of life where we are directly touched by the Spirit of God that elicits the cry of the psalmist: 'I praise you, for I am awesomely and wonderfully designed' (Ps 139:14).

Ethical Living[5]

Paul teaches not only fundamental truths about the Christ-event and its meaning for human life, but also exhorts Christians to upright ethical conduct in this life, in the 'in-between'. The Christian who believes and is baptised has been energised by the Spirit (Rm 8:14) and can no longer live a merely natural life but lives by the law of love. Paul's exhortations for the most part consist of lists of virtues and vices that should or should not characterise the Christian life as well as lists of duties for members of the Christian household. He also lists prayer and asceticism because Christians live in the presence of God and have a duty of communing with him in adoration, praise, thanksgiving and supplication.

The morality of the new covenant is a morality of love, summed up in love of God and neighbour. To be able to live this life of love in the Spirit on a daily basis, however, requires moral instruction to educate the conscience as to what loving means concretely. For the Christian's response to God's call consists first of all in submission to the loving activity of the Spirit, but this also includes compliance with God's will contained in the traditions of the believing community that are expressed in hortatory sections of Paul's letters. God's demand confronts the Christian both in the internal impulse of the Spirit to do the loving thing, and also in the external word of the Church's exhortation which concretises that impulse, for both are an integral part of the Good News.

> Christian morality is indeed resumed in love of neighbour, but it is not *reduced* to it, if by that we mean that love of neighbour competes with, overrides or replaces the particular demands which confront the Christian in virtue of his total situation.[6]

While the new covenant morality is a morality of the Spirit, it is to be lived out concretely in the Church and in the world. It is an *incarnate* morality. Therefore, the early Christians looked to Paul for guidance in living the new life of the Spirit. A sure sign that the Christian is guided by the Spirit is his willingness to comply with the directives of external authority in the community. The reason for this is that love of itself is not a sufficiently articulated ethical norm for guiding Christians in the many and often complex circumstances of daily living. External guidance protects love from degenerating into subjectivism, sentimentality or self-deception to which even believers are exposed, not because they are evil people, but simply because they are human beings. It should not surprise us that, from the beginning, believers submitted their love to external direction.

Paul's understanding of the Christian's situation in the Spirit and in the human, social reality of the world enabled him to elaborate an ethic of the Spirit that remained incarnate and achieved a balance between love and law, spontaneity and principle, and inward and outward word. Since Christ is the only authentic human being, a Christ-like existence is extended to humans in the context of a community ruled both by the Spirit and the external word of those placed in authority over it by the same Spirit. The apostle is also aware that believers live in a civil and political society that is not wholly oriented to the same goals as the Christian community. Although they are citizens of a heavenly 'commonwealth' (Phil 3:20), Christians have obligations in this earthly life that need to be met. Paul's explanation of the meaning of the Christ-event will be further developed in the Church's dogmatic tradition throughout the centuries. His ethical vision will be deepened in her moral tradition. The result is a profound understanding of Christ in his mysteries and a coherent ethical vision to guide Christian living in the world.

Church's Self-Understanding

The Church is the instrument willed by God and commanded by the risen Christ (Mt 28:18–20) to fulfil God's saving will for all humankind and so it is missionary of its very nature. It transcends local cultures, yet each local community (diocese) is the Church of

God. It witnesses to the eschatological hope of fulfilment beyond history as the final destiny of humanity.

The reign of God has not only its own time, but also its own place in the new Israel gathered around Jesus, symbolised by the twelve disciples as representatives of the twelve tribes of Israel. There, it is visible and tangible. It is God's rule, revealed first of all in a renewed Israel and through it to the nations – a visible community where the ultimate rule of God is evident in a people who serve God alone. The reign of God must have a *people*; it is not something individualistic or merely spiritual. It happens within the community of disciples that is defined by mutual love, service, forgiveness, non-retaliation, etc., as illustrated, for example, in the Sermon on the Mount. The Church is the sign or sacrament of the reign of God in the process of becoming a reality within history and will reach completion in the general resurrection at the end of time. The visible sign of this reign is also an *effective* sign, tangible and identifiable, where one can hear the gospel, receive the sacraments and participate in the life of the renewed people of God. Discipleship is a sharing in the life of Jesus, a whole new way of life that is *freely* accepted. It requires a new style of living, a new community of persons to witness to it by their believing life together.

The Church becomes the carrier of this new truth in history through the gospel writers who offered their stories as a true understanding of the real world. They believed that it is the providence of God that rules history – that God is saving his people in history (past), that the Spirit guides their life (in the present) and gives the hope of eternal life (in the future). To avail of this new truth, participation in Church life is essential – worship, prayer, sacraments, service to others and witness. The Church may be compared to a human body with different parts – charisms given by the Spirit for the common good (1 Cor 12) to promote holiness of life.

Through conversion, repentance, faith, baptism and membership of the Christian community, it becomes possible to live this new kind of life more in keeping with what God wants when we allow ourselves to be guided by his Spirit and live a morality of love (1 Cor.13). It is here that we discover the full truth of our humanity, witnessed to in a striking way by the saints. Christian theology gives a clearer articulation of this truth, while the Church itself as an institution witnesses to the end of society beyond history. It is the place of communion with God with its own structure, separated from political society with which it lives in a certain tension. Since it claims to have a true understanding of what it means to be human, the Church can help in the right ordering of human living in community. In addition, Church and State have their rightful place in society and a proper balance between them ensures freedom – not freedom from all restraints, which is mere fantasy, but freedom for doing the good, the true, the just and the loving thing that would ensure human well-being and flourishing, peace and happiness.

We look to the Church's self-interpretation in its liturgical life, service and teaching to find truth as a mode of living the mystery of reality rather than looking for definitive answers to questions we may have. Truth may then be regarded as a person's recognition of one's finitude and creatureliness oriented to supreme Truth that is best exemplified in the saints who become our models. Faith also seeks understanding to show its reasonableness, an articulation of the Truth itself as the answer to the questions of being and truth posed by human beings. This is the role of theology, which uses language symbols applied analogically to speak of unseen realities. Thus the symbol 'grace', for example, connotes God's intrusion into human life that transforms it into living in hope of future fulfilment. A mature faith is animated from within by a love of God that leads to friendship with God, and theology becomes the depository of religious experiences amassed by the Church through the centuries. The *Catechism of the Catholic Church* contains the authentic content of what Christians believe, celebrate, live and pray.

Church in the World

The Church is not primarily a political institution built to promote social equality, justice and peace. It is the community of Christ's followers, freely embraced, that is led by the Spirit and accommodates itself to living in the world in time and space. This inevitably gives rise to problems of adjustment and compromises, failures and lapses, as is evident from the Pauline exhortations. Reciprocal love modelled on that of Jesus makes for authentic Christians by shaping their lives, behaviour and personalities. In this way, the Church becomes the carrier of the Good News of Jesus Christ to the nations across time and space. The Church is a place of deliverance from a world alienated from God as well as a locus of communion with God. There is an inevitable tension between it and a world in rebellion against God, yet called to salvation under Christ. This gives rise to the battle between good and evil in daily life. The Church is also the corporate understanding of what it means to be human by enabling a new lifestyle to be lived in the world that is concerned with the right order of living and so bears witness to the truth about humanity.

The absence of the Church in society then would lead to profound cultural and spiritual impoverishment in the social and moral spheres of life. Living independently of political systems, the Church is the sign and safeguard of the transcendence of the person and prevents an untimely closure of the world against its promised destiny beyond history. When the Church becomes the State, freedom is lost; when the Church is eliminated as a public and relevant authority, freedom is also extinguished because the State claims for itself the justification of morality. In modern times this has taken the form of ideological authority. The State then becomes the party and, since there is no longer any other authority of equal rank, it becomes totalitarian when not balanced by a publicly recognised authority of conscience.

> The existence of a new society that does not coincide with the state is a fundamental factor in the liberation of man. Wherever this distinction is revoked, an essential sphere of freedom is lost, for then the state has to proceed again to regulate the whole of human life. It again draws the realm of the divine to itself, because it again becomes the bearer of religion. It thereby destroys that freedom of conscience which rests on the position of the new society of faith vis-à-vis the state. The distinction, consequent upon Christianity, between the universal religious community and the necessarily particular civil community in no way means a complete separation of the two realms so that religion would now withdraw into the merely spiritual and the state would be reduced to a purely political pragmatism without ethical orientation.[8]

As a community of believers participating in the life of God, the Church breaks down barriers between heaven and earth. It guards against reducing people to what they can achieve by themselves by its emphasis on being over doing. The Church will offer resistance only when the State demands rejection of God or commands evil, otherwise it will cooperate in doing good for all. Since the State is no longer the bearer of religious authority that binds conscience, the Church becomes the moral authority that directs human living. On the balance of the relationship between Church and State depends freedom from tyranny of every kind and so the fight for Christianity in the public square is a fight for human dignity and freedom as well.

Endnotes

1   Raymond E. Brown, 'Part III: The Pauline Letters,' in *An Introduction to the New Testament*, New York: Doubleday, 1997, pp. 407–680. See also, James D.G. Dunn, *The Theology of Paul the Apostle*, Edinburgh: T&T Clark, 1998.

2   David Stanley, 'Christ, the Last Adam,' in Michael J. Taylor (ed.), *A Companion to Paul: Readings in Pauline Theology*, New York: Alba House, 1975, p. 16.

3   C.F.D. Moule, 'St Paul and Dualism: The Pauline Conception of Resurrection', *New Testament Studies*, 12/2 (1966), p. 107.

4   Joseph Ratzinger, *Principles of Catholic Theology*, San Francisco: Ignatius Press, 2012, pp. 184–185.

5   Here I draw upon the excellent work in T.J. Deidun, *New Covenant Morality in Paul*, Rome: Biblical Institute Press, 1981, pp. 156–226.

6   *Ibid.*, p. 185.

7   For the following, I am indebted to Joseph Ratzinger, *Church, Ecumenism, and Politics*, San Francisco: Ignatius Press, 1987, pp. 175–255.

8   *Ibid.*, pp. 251–252.

CHAPTER TWELVE:
HUMAN CHARACTERISTICS

Introduction[1]

The natural sciences are part of the human quest for understanding the truth of our humanity because we are at least partly at home in the material universe. The world must be meaningful since both philosophy and revelation testify to the de-divinisation of the mythic cosmos; the Creator becomes transcendent, and the world is regarded as created and contingent, thereby creating the possibility of science. Science sets out to explain how the different levels of being in the cosmos came about. Its methodology, however, is not the only criterion for every inquiry. Science operates best as complementary to the other sources of truth, as John Paul II in a message to the director of the Vatican Observatory observed:

> Science can purify religion from error and superstition; religion can purify science from idolatry and false absolutes. Each can help the other to enter into a more complete world, where both can prosper.[2]

Human beings belong, yet do not fully belong, to what preceded them in the course of evolution beginning with the Big Bang some 13.7 billion years ago. There is an unbridgeable gap between us and sub-human creatures. Homo sapiens differ not only in degree, but also in kind from other creatures, as we are separated by an enormous cognitive barrier. The human species is an entirely unprecedented entity on the world scene, appearing perhaps about 150,000 years ago from a common ancestor we all share as human beings, as indicated by a fundamental similarity in our anatomy.

Humans have genetic origins that result in a body configuration with a human brain and vocal tract which form the material foundations of human consciousness, language, understanding and freedom.[3] Human symbolisation, though, is something entirely new. Symbols externalise for others acts of the human subject (e.g. affection, understanding, judgment) that serve a purpose different from biological needs. The very question of meaning for human beings arises from the experience of reality itself. Symbols convey truth experienced about transcendent reality, that is, a *consciousness* of participation in something beyond what can be perceived in the material world. The truth expressed in symbols belongs to transcendent experience that is expressed in myths, philosophy, revelation and mystical symbols.

Human beings who experience reality can, therefore, express themselves through various symbols. What remains is the constancy of human nature in its search for order in existence, as well as attunement to the cosmic order. They can voice this awareness through language symbols that then become the means by which reality reveals itself and, consequently, becomes the carrier of meaning, which is different from animal communication. Furthermore, human language is characterised by self-awareness of both speaker and listener and cannot adequately be accounted for by the natural sciences.

Human beings have also a capacity for truth and goodness, which we call the soul, the locus of sentience, reason and will, and so human understanding must be grasped on its own terms. Bernard Lonergan discusses the human activities of experiencing, understanding and judging that refer to objects given at both the sense and intellectual levels of questioning.[4] It seems, then, that human beings recognise not only objects studied by the natural sciences, but also the internal experience of themselves and their actions. Furthermore, there is the specifically human activity of living in the truth, that is, the conformity or correspondence of affirmation or negation to what is and what is not.[5] Humans can even put truth above the desire to survive, as in the case of martyrdom. There is not only the human desire for truth, but also the human desire to avoid truth by a counter-truth, or what we call the lie. Only in humans is such self-consciousness encountered, together with the quest for truth and the choice of the lie.

Furthermore, humans experience a freedom which not only excludes necessity, but also includes the positive aspect of responsibility when consciousness becomes conscience.[6] In and through our choices we make ourselves what we are and what we will become. Each person must decide for oneself whether to be good or evil since we cannot escape from moral reflection. As Aleksandr Solzhenitsyn reminds us, 'the dividing line between good and evil cuts through the heart of every human being.' Since our freedom is disclosed in our choices, it can only be discovered through the way we actually live our lives.

It seems, therefore, that to understand human existence, we must move beyond the natural sciences to properly explain the phenomena of language, understanding and freedom in human beings. We live in a material world but do not entirely belong to it. For human consciousness transcends space and time to reach out to limitless horizons of beauty, meaning, truth and goodness which usually happen within an inter-personal setting.

Humans as Relational Beings

Human beings are fundamentally orientated to seeking and finding love that is typically relational and includes the following interrelated facets:

> Myself as intrinsically relational or youwards, how I live that youwardness by sacrificing myself for you, and how, if that self-giving is reciprocated, we become persons in communion, moving from youwardness to wewardness.[7]

In fact, all the things that are most important to who I am, I have received from others, beginning with my very existence. Since my whole existence is a *gift*, I must be prepared to share that gift unconditionally. Paradoxically, in making myself a gift for others, I achieve personal fulfilment through losing my freedom in communion:

So I'd suggest that the answer to the question 'who am I' would be in the direction of, 'I am a being capable of being in communion with others.' Of course, as free, I can choose not to be in communion.[8]

Each human being as well as being a unity is also unique and so cannot be substituted for. Human embryos are, from the first moment of conception, human beings who share an identity with the older human beings they grow up to become. Humans, though, cannot be defined like things in the world, because, although they exist in time, they participate in what is beyond time. And so we have to correct our tendency to speak of humans as if they were only material beings, for unlike other things in the universe, human beings have a broader horizon beyond the material.

> We can say, then, that a human person is a unique embodied identity intrinsically oriented to communion with others, where the authentic unfolding of that capacity for unlimited, self-sacrificing love requires a readiness to lose ourselves for the sake of the other.[9]

The coming into existence of human beings passes through a long evolutionary sequence, but this is not the complete explanation. There is also the development of the individual organism from embryo to adulthood that cannot adequately be classified as an organism. Scientific evidence supports the conclusion that the zygote (single-celled organism) is a human organism and a new human being from the moment of conception and that it controls from the beginning the forming of structures and relationships required to continue developing to a mature state. Since it comes from human parents, the zygote must be human and not merely a zoological entity. It is the essential material embodiment of a human being as it unfolds in the womb with still dormant capacities for beauty, truth, meaning, goodness and personal relationships. Embryonic development is the material unfolding of a specifically human existence – matter specially disposed to encapsulate the human soul, of which such a soul is its substantial form (*anima forma corporis*, Aquinas).

Humans as Transcendent Beings

Human beings are not autonomous, independent beings, but the creation of a higher, personal being we call God, together with parents as co-creators. They do not possess the origin and basis of their own being. Existence is an act of graciousness on God's part and so humans are essentially God-related creatures ('image and likeness', Gn 1:26). The basis of this unique human dignity is the fact that humans can dialogue with God. In the New Testament, anthropology is linked to Christology; Christ becomes the authentic human being and Adamic humanity is remodelled in the image of Christ. United with Christ in life and in death, human beings will live forever in the presence of God. Since Christ revealed God as a loving Father, humanity's response-oriented existence becomes a dialogue of love.

For Christ to become a reality in our world today, inner conversion is necessary to allow oneself to be liberated from an alienated existence in order to grow to full human stature: 'To mature manhood, to the measure of the stature of the fulness of Christ' (Eph 4:13). Human fulfilment takes place not in isolation, but in community with Christ, the Spirit and other believers. There is a tension between the already and the not yet, for Christians walk by faith, not by sight, in the hope of things that lie hidden in the future, especially in the face of suffering and death. Resurrection from the dead is the Christian answer to the incompleteness of human existence as lived and experienced in the in-between of birth and death, but destined for a glorified life with God beyond the grave. In Christ, God lovingly reaches down to humans in response to their existential search in order to raise them up to himself. This expression of love is to make humans into what God originally meant them to be.

We have reviewed elements of a biblical anthropology and have seen that the vocabulary employed expresses the whole person under various aspects. This is quite different from the now common understanding which views body and soul as two separate components of human beings. The Bible does not regard human beings as autonomous and distinct entities, but as dependent on and related to God and to one another as persons. Paradoxically, this radical dependence on God is the human being's great liberation from fear of the world and the cosmic powers that constituted the source of mythical thinking. Human existence is essentially a verbal, dialogical one. It is a response-giving existence in freedom. Humans are addressed by God and called to respond to him. Because of its unified conception of human beings, the Old Testament was able to give a positive evaluation of man's corporeal, material existence. This explains the strong Old Testament orientation towards earthly existence and the lack of any clear articulation of an afterlife until relatively late in its history.

Nevertheless, the Old Testament idea of humanity is incomplete. It has yet to await the coming of God in the person of Jesus Christ in order to fully reveal its true nature and be rescued from the sense of alienation experienced in living. That is why biblical anthropology becomes inseparable from Christology in the New Testament. The authentic human being is Jesus Christ. And so, Adamic humanity, remodelled in the image of Christ, has already planted in its heart the seed of immortality. Still living in the 'in-between,' believers must allow themselves to 'put on' Christ in order to be re-made in the image of their Creator. United with Christ in death, believers will become a body of glory to live forever in the presence of God for all eternity.

We have viewed revelation within the larger context of human experience and advancement in consciousness. Humans seek to reach out to participate in the goodness of God, and this creates order in the world (as elaborated in Greek philosophy). Christ becomes the most profound realisation of human participation in the divine pull or invitation. In him, our attunement to God reaches its maximum perfection through grace in death. Christians, therefore, are pilgrims on a journey to the fulness of life that is now lived in faith, hope and love. This is the truth about human beings, of history and its order. Christianity is a primary means by which modern people can regain contact with the source of existential order. It illuminates consciousness and, through language symbols, articulates spiritual experiences of participation in being. There is a link between consciousness and language symbolisation because humans participate in a reality which is mysterious and lived in between life and death. Humans ask questions and articulate their experiences intelligibly in language symbols. Consciousness links experience and symbolisation that ranges from compactness to differentiation to give gradations of clarity and illumination concerning the truth of the human condition (successively in mythology, non-Christian religions, philosophy and revelation). The unknown God (Acts 17:23) who searches for and draws human beings to himself is revealed by Jesus Christ as the ground of being. We must therefore go beyond a consciousness that restricts itself to objects in the material world because experiences of transcendence and their symbolisation are, as a matter of fact, part of the history of humanity as well. When we neglect these, we replace reality with a succession of dream worlds, or ideologies, which in turn degenerate into existence in rebellion against God and human beings that is so much in evidence today. Christ opens the way to the fulness of life. Those who follow him are already being transfigured within history through struggle and suffering that prepare them for participation in the life of God who is love.

Endnotes

1   For a fresh and comprehensive guide to understanding who we are as human beings, see Brendan Purcell, *From Big Bang to Big Mystery: Human Origins in the Light of Creation and Evolution,* Dublin: Veritas, 2011. It combines the latest in scientific thinking with philosophy and revelation to offer a new synthesis on what it means to be human.

2   John Paul II, Letter to Reverend George V. Coyne SJ, Director of the Vatican Observatory, 1988. https://www.vatican.va/content/john-paul-ii/en/letters/1988/documents/hf_jp-ii_let_19880601_padre-coyne.html; accessed on 12 November 2021.

3   Purcell, *From Big Bang to Big Mystery,* pp. 189–332.

4   B.J.F. Lonergan, *Insight: A Study of Human Understanding,* London: Longmans, 1961; *Method in Theology,* London: Darton, Longman & Todd, 1972.

5   Lonergan, *Insight,* p. 552.

6   Lonergan, *Collection,* New York: Herder & Herder, 1967, pp. 237–238.

7   Purcell, *op. cit.*, p. 295.

8   *Ibid.*, p. 300.

9   *Ibid.*, p. 305.

CONCLUSION

History as Epiphany of Divine Presence[1]

The question of meaning keeps arising from humanity's experience of reality from time immemorial. Different cultures expressed this quest in myth, non-Christian religions, philosophy and revelation because gifted individuals in these cultures were able to transcend the particular times and places in which they flourished. Eric Voegelin speaks of 'spiritual outbursts' in the great Eastern religious experiences as well as in the more differentiated ones in Greek philosophy, in Israel and in Christianity that were followed by developments and regressions which have characterised Western culture. A deep unity in diversity can be envisaged for the whole of humanity. History, then, may be regarded as the relationship between each human person, between communities of persons, in each society and culture, and between persons and societies with the God that grounds them. This becomes the foundation for the creation of a universal dialogue that reaches out in a genuine search for truth, justice and love to those who are different from us.

The meaning of history at it deepest core is, therefore, the disclosure of God's presence manifested in human consciousness in the foundational experiences and symbolisations of divine presence. Language symbols attempt to express the presence with humans of an essentially hidden God, the frontier of whose presence becomes luminous through revelation. This was already perceived and expressed dimly in mythical imagination and reached greater clarity successively in the symbolisations of non-Christian religions, Greek philosophy and biblical revelation, culminating in Jesus as the image (*eikon*) of the unseen God (Col 1:15). We may then speak of revelation in a twofold sense: the gradual awareness of the presence of God to humans throughout the course of history; and the distinct symbolic form of biblical revelation. Myths, non-Christian religions and philosophy in their ideas, practices and gestures express the human search for God who is unknown and unseen, although experienced everywhere as present throughout the course of human history. The uniqueness of Judeo-Christianity is that God comes to meet us *personally* by encountering us at our level in order to save us. Christ becomes the locus of human encounter with the true God, Creator and Saviour of the world.

This, then, is the biblical vision of human beings and their history. Human nature is not something closed in on itself but limitlessly open to and oriented towards the transcendent reality of a personal, loving God who has drawn near to us in Christ. A relationship with God is, therefore, an integral element of the human spirit: 'You have made us for yourself, and our heart is restless until it rests in you.'[2] Human beings can only be fulfilled and satisfied by God alone. In the Incarnation it is not human beings searching and reaching up to God, but God stooping down in loving concern and graciousness to embrace human existence in order to raise it up to participate in divinity, thereby making human beings into what God intended them to become from the beginning.

Numinous Experience

An interior awareness of transcendent reality has been experienced by many people in vastly different cultures, revealing an almost universal presence throughout the course of history. This awareness must have a common root. Why do people feel called to worship both privately and publicly? It seems that this interior awareness comes from a divine source because it is not controllable by human beings and has a dimension that is trans-physical. It is the sense of something mysterious, powerful, spiritual and overwhelming that elicits humility, recognition of creatureliness and submission, but also of something fascinating, desirable and good. This is the foundation of all religions throughout the world, evoking a sense of mystery that gives rise to wonder, astonishment and amazement, but also of something that is wholly other. All major religions attribute these qualities to what we Christians call God. These attributes create strong impressions that cause people to seek, desire and value sacred and religious symbols, community, worship and revelation in order to find a higher sense of fulfilment. It seems, then, that the human being is by nature '*homo religiosus*'.

The transcendent reality is experienced as loving and oriented towards relationships. Several common characteristics of this reality are found among world religions in varying degrees, for example: transcendent and holy; immanent in human awareness; is the highest truth; good, loving and beautiful; the way to it requires ethical discipline, prayer and asceticism; includes service towards others; the highest way to eternal happiness is through love. Fragments of these are evident in all the major religions to a greater or lesser extent. It seems, then, that God is sensed as present in some manner to human beings throughout history inviting them to himself, a God who is relational and consequently personal.

Experience of the Sacred

Religion originates from experience of the 'numinous' and expresses itself outwardly through myths, rituals, symbols and sacred communities as openings to connecting with transcendent reality. All religions believe that transcendent reality has broken into our world in the form of hierophanies or theophanies that separate the sacred from the profane. Sacred times, places, rituals and myths help relive this original experience. They tell participants how to live and develop character for living in a purposeful manner. Over the course of four millennia, most people have sought the sacred in order to be taught lessons about purpose in life, evil to be avoided, good to be done and virtues and laws to guard it.

All of this is hardly a chance occurrence or the result of some natural or physical cause; it is more likely to be the result of the presence of transcendent reality within them. Consequently, it should not be surprising that there are similarities between religions: awareness of and desire for the sacred and fulfilment by it; sacred times and places; myths, rituals and symbols. Human beings have made religion the source of reality and of meaning. They have moved from numinous experience to religion, that is, communities which seek expression in sacred times and places, rituals, sacred writings, myths and symbols. A common interior experience develops into common beliefs and expressions in the different religions. Historically, practically everyone was religious in some form or other. Today, some sixteen percent of modern people, mostly in the Western world, claim to be irreligious. This gives rise to anxiety, lack of meaning, angst, alienation from self and reality that is experienced as loneliness and guilt and an increase in impulsivity, aggression, lawlessness and substance abuse. Western culture seems to be heading for a crisis with its loss of hope for the future. This crisis manifests itself in superficiality, materialism, autonomy and self-indulgence, revealing thereby its lack of purpose and identity. It seems that transcendence is an inescapable feature of every person, which explains the heightened anxiety when it is not acknowledged. Human beings become aware of good and evil through conscience – attraction to the good, repulsion towards evil and the idea of moral obligation suggests the presence of God as an authoritative voice bidding people to do certain things and avoid others.

Desire for Perfection

Human beings naturally seek the perfect, unconditional and unrestricted that invites them to look for greater truth, goodness, love, beauty and harmony beyond what they have already discovered, namely, a transcendent horizon implying that human beings too are transcendent. These desires not only point to our transcendent nature and trans-physical soul, but also to our ultimate happiness, purpose in life, fulfilment and destiny. They are the most important capacities or powers within us. For example, we seek to know everything about everything; we want the complete and perfect answer. We desire to know but we cannot desire what we are not aware of. It seems then that God must somehow be present to our consciousness, inviting us to explore reality. The totality of reality must include a necessary reality we call God, for there is a tacit intuition by humans that reality is intelligible. We seek perfect love and have a sense of it when we falsely expect that imperfect humans can provide unconditional love. But we cannot recognise imperfection unless we have some idea of what perfection is. This recognition does not come from the world or people who are themselves imperfect.

Human beings also desire perfect goodness or justice. We have a sense of what this perfection would be like and when we fail to find it, we express outrage toward social structures or groups. We look for a more perfect social order, justice system, equality or idealism. We are aware of imperfections, so we must have some inkling of what perfect justice and its effect on individuals, groups, communities, societies or states would be. When God gives us this yearning and capacity for perfect justice, he reveals himself as perfectly just. There is also the awareness of a desire for beauty and the recognition of its imperfections in this world that spurs us on to improvement in arts, architecture, music, drama, literature, etc. We have an ideal of perfect beauty and the capacity to recognise imperfection. Beautiful objects evoke delight, enjoyment and point beyond themselves. God is seemingly calling us to himself in our yearning for perfect beauty. We also desire perfect harmony, the feeling of being completely at home, which is not possible in this world.

It seems, then, that by the light of reason alone we can come to know what kind of revelation we would be looking for – one that is consistent with the perfection of these desires. Love is regarded universally as the ultimate fulfilment of our capacity for self-transcendence. Desire for perfect truth is the beginning and perfect love is the end, and so we gain a greater insight into the mind and heart of God as a result. When we attend to rational reflection on our transcendent awareness and desires, we conclude to the existence of a unique being who is also perfect love, truth, goodness, beauty and harmony and the source of these desires within us. Reality is, therefore, intelligible and leads to acknowledging the existence of God, the Creator of all and source of our tacit awareness of our desire for perfection. This God is not only present to us, but also desires to be in relationship with us. He is not only the source of truth, but also love, goodness and beauty. For the source of our desire for perfection must be God who attracts us with his transcendent powerful presence – an invitation to a life of virtue to attain our highest purpose, dignity and destiny in perfect goodness and love.

The Soul

The realisation that we are more than material beings and possess a unique transcendent soul is important for defining life's purpose and destiny and resisting the materialism that is so widespread today. The evidence of near-death experiences suggests that consciousness has a trans-physical ground apart from the brain, that it can exist apart from the body and even survive death. The soul is the mediator between consciousness and the transcendent and explains our capacity to pursue complete truth and the other transcendentals. The trans-physical activities of the soul and its contents affect the way we see ourselves, the meaning of life, our dignity and destiny. If we ignore these promptings, we reduce ourselves to the temporal and material and become disconnected from our transcendent purpose and destiny.

External Evidence

Scientific research tells us that the universe had a beginning and so there must be something that caused it to exist. For the universe could not have moved itself from nothing to something before the beginning. The Big Bang theory states that the universe came into being at a particular moment (13.7 billion years ago) and points to a Creator. There are also time-honoured logical proofs for the existence of God in metaphysics known as the Five Proofs that reach back to Plato, Aristotle and Thomas Aquinas. The conclusion from both science and metaphysics is the high probability of a Creator. New evidence for God and creation has also come to light from physics, mathematics and philosophy in recent decades that counteracts the prevailing agnosticism and atheism in scientific circles. These discoveries together with the traditional proofs of God's existence provide a rational foundation for the existence of a unique, super-intelligent Creator of all that exists.

Conclusion

If all of this is true, then we would want to know how to relate to this transcendent being. If God is perfectly good and loving, it is unlikely that he would leave us with unanswered questions and incapable of reaching our transcendent destiny to which he seems to be calling us. Consequently, it is probable that there is some exterior revelation to complement all these interior yearnings. Would God want to make a personal revelation to us as well as through personal intermediaries, prophets and holy men? If so, then God would have to make himself subject to the limitations of time, culture and a particular place. The radical claim of Christianity is that God sent his Son into the world to reveal the true God in word and deed, culminating in a self-sacrificing act of love. It was God who prepared both Jews and Gentiles through revelation and philosophy that would be necessary to interpret and understand him. Christianity, then, seems to be the best candidate to show God's compassionate love. It can be shown that this revelation is connected with God and that it fulfils and completes the other world religions.

Non-Christian Religions and Christianity[3]

Non-Christian Religions

Pope Benedict XVI called for a reasoned dialogue with the great world religions. Since the mid-1960s, the Catholic Church has developed a positive and critical approach towards them. It is open to whatever truth, goodness and beauty is discovered in the non-Christian religions and cultures of the world which would challenge Christians to become more faithful to God in their own living of the Christian life. It also wishes to work together with adherents of world religions to establish justice and peace in our troubled world and seek to build bridges between all peoples since our common humanity is marked by God's image.

Non-Christian religions embody sacred rites, rules of life and doctrines as ways of responding to what transcends human beings. By these means, people are enabled to come in contact with the Divine through openness in faith and love. There is a seeking and being drawn prompted by God in their concrete situations because God wishes all people of goodwill to be saved and come to knowledge of the truth (1 Tm 2:4). The various religions represent both the effort of human beings in seeking God throughout the entire history of humankind and, more importantly, the diverse ways in which God first sets out in search of them. Nevertheless, these religions are inherently ambiguous.

On the one hand, non-Christian religions are the development of the natural desire to make contact with the transcendent which Paul observed during his visit to Athens:

> I noticed, as I strolled round admiring your sacred monuments, that you had an altar inscribed 'To an Unknown God'. Well, the God whom I proclaim is the one you already worship without knowing it. (Acts 17:23)

God attracts through reason, conscience and natural law and can use any situation to touch people who sincerely seek the truth in their non-Christian religious milieu.

On the other hand, the adherents of these religions are also immersed in situations of evil, sin and idolatry, and so their knowledge of God is often distorted, obscured, overlaid with error and demonic: 'The gods of the nations are demons' (Ps 96:5, LXX). In Romans 1:18–32, Paul describes the pagan existential situation; their refusal to acknowledge God led to all kinds of immorality and perversion. Pagan deities inspire fear, terror, dread and anxiety. These give rise to idolatry, magic, sorcery and even human sacrifice to appease them. 'What pagans sacrifice they offer to demons not to God. I do not want you to be partners with demons' (1 Cor 10:20; cf. Rev 2:14, 20). There is, then, a mixture of truth, falsehood and moral depravity in non-Christian religions that calls for careful discernment.

Objectively, these religions are incomplete and unfinished ways of salvation and need purification, but this does not include any judgment about the sanctification of particular individuals within them in ways that are known only to God. It can be said that, historically and concretely, God's grace normally encounters individuals, not only in the intimacy of their conscience but also within their total socio-cultural situation. Individuals live their religious lives in the forms proposed to them through their religious communities. They can be saved in their religions but by means of the grace of Christ working though the Spirit beyond the confines of the visible Church. For only in Christ as God-with-us is found God's full self-disclosure and the complete means of salvation for which all people are unconsciously seeking: 'For there is only one God, and there is only one mediator between God and mankind, himself a man, Christ Jesus, who sacrificed himself as a ransom for them all' (1 Tm 2:5). There are no parallel or alternate ways of salvation. Jesus alone saves us through the Spirit who is not confined within the boundaries of the Church. That is why, during the course of history, non-Christian religions have incorporated a large amount of meditations, illuminations, spiritual experiences, prayers and fidelity. God has allowed himself to be glimpsed, however imperfectly, through these religions. Paul, in his speech to the Athenians, presupposed some knowledge, however vague, of the mystery of salvation which he then explicitly proclaims to them (Acts 17:24–31).

God also speaks through historical events. In the life of each individual there are various encounters and events that have a profound emotional significance, for example, experiences of birth, death, love, kindness, etc. God can speak through them in a wordless but intelligible way. A person can hear in these experiences questions about the meaning of life or an invitation to go out to something greater than oneself. What is true of individuals is also true of communities, tribes, peoples and nations. In the vicissitudes of history such groups are faced time and again with the religious question. There is a process of education going on leading to a state of preparedness for the reception of the gospel. Only in a groping way, though, do the non-Christian religions suggest the mystery of salvation and the radical conversion from selfishness that is necessary when compared to the perfect expression of divine truth revealed in the person of Jesus Christ. In Christ and through Christ all things have been created (1 Cor 8:6; Col 1:16). There is only one sure way of salvation willed by God from all eternity in Christ, and in this the teachings of the philosophers and the non-Christian religions are somehow included. God's goodness is at work among the nations from the very beginning (Gn 1–11). However, this in no way diminishes the necessity and urgency of the Church's missionary outreach to the nations commanded by Christ (Mt 28:19–20).

With the advent of Christianity there is the possibility of helping our contemporaries escape the hopeless alternative of shutting themselves off from the modern age or fully capitulating to it. The

Church's missionary outreach to them and to the nations is, then, a manifestation of God's will, the advance party of a new universal humanity through her proclamation. The Church becomes the locus of unity and reconciliation.

Christianity

Christianity is not based on mythical or philosophical speculation; it is concerned with a divine historical event and presence in the world that can be perceived by a rational analysis of reality – a God who speaks and acts. It may be regarded as the perfect philosophy (Justin) that has attained to the truth and is at the same time practical as the art of living and dying aright, something that can only be done successfully in the light of truth. It is a synthesis of reason, faith and life, for human beings can rightly be understood only in relation to God. Only God's self-revelation can answer questions humans have regarding their transcendent destiny.

If God is good and loving as we have seen, he would want to reveal himself to us in our incompleteness as a *personal* revelation. Christianity would be a major candidate for this revelation because of its claim that God is unconditional love and that he has sent his Son into the world. God's love and care were already revealed to Israel and in a Greek culture that optimised the use of reason. This would provide the rational infrastructure to help spread the Good News initially throughout the Roman Empire and subsequently to all peoples of all times and places.

Jesus reveals God as a loving Father (*Abba*) and compared him to the father in the parable of the prodigal son (Lk 15:11–32). Jesus demonstrated that he himself is unconditional love, especially in his self-sacrifice, anticipated at the Last Supper and consummated on Calvary. The resurrection proved that he is indeed Emmanuel, God-with-us. He formed disciples and, after his resurrection, gave them his Spirit to accompany them on mission. This is convincing evidence but in itself is not sufficient. A movement of the heart on the part of the seeker is necessary. A desire to be healed and saved by Jesus requires a *decision* to accept him as Lord and Saviour. This faith will transform and enhance our nature, dignity and destiny as well as showing us how to live and die. We will also want to profess our faith within the Christian community and share it with others.

Faith

Faith is not primarily knowledge, but an existential decision to trust that God will give us a future beyond the frontiers of death. It has its origin in God reaching out to human beings beginning with Abraham and through the people of Israel to the person of Jesus Christ, the Word made flesh. This faith is based on revelation that is mediated to us through the Church. It is a view of reality given to those who trust, hope and love and is something more basic than knowledge – an existential attitude, a fundamental decision about the direction of one's life: 'I believe you, Jesus of Nazareth; I believe that in you was revealed that divine purpose which allows me to live with confidence, tranquillity, patience, and courage.'[4] This attitude is best exemplified by people who have lived it out, for example, the saints.

The Bible describes the first stage in the history of faith. Abraham is the great exemplary figure who set out on a journey at the end of which stands the figure of Jesus of Nazareth. He let go of what was safe and familiar in response to a call from God and placed his future in God's hands. He lived his life in a spirit of trust against all appearances because he believed that God would take care of his future that was symbolised concretely in posterity and land. According to Paul, faith in Jesus Christ is a continuation of the faith of Abraham (Rm 4:1–25). Christian faith also trusts in God who raised Jesus Christ from the dead and promises a future which crosses the threshold of death to an eternal future life with God.

> Thus, in the last analysis believing, trusting, and loving are one, and all the theses around which belief revolves are only concrete expressions of the all-embracing about-turn, of the assertion 'I believe in you' – of the discovery of God in the countenance of the man Jesus of Nazareth.[5]

Primacy of Love

Love is universally recognised as an essential part of one's happiness and fulfilment with an unconditionally loving God. Jesus claimed to bring the definitive revelation about love of God, which he demonstrated in word and action. What is love? Jesus himself described the interior attributes of love in the beatitudes (Mt 5:3–11) and St Paul lists attitudes and behaviours central to love (1 Cor 13:4–8). There are, then, three dimensions to love: attitudes to free us from self-centredness; attitudes that recognise the intrinsic dignity of others; and attitudes and acts of compassion and service. These are illustrated and encapsulated in the parable of the Good Samaritan (Lk 10:25–37). We need the grace of God to inspire and guide us in deepening our love for others. Such love has the power to heal individuals, communities, society and cultures. If we accept this with our minds, we must enter into the mystery of Jesus with our hearts to be able to recognise his love for us *personally*. Jesus proclaimed God's unconditional love, but we must want it enough to make it our own by deciding to follow the way of Jesus in his Church guided by the Spirit.

Jesus' love was shown in his healings, exorcisms, friendship with sinners, care for the poor and outcasts and in his relationship with his disciples. His mission, though, was not to take away suffering, but to use it as a means of preparation for the kingdom and eternal life both for oneself and for others. In the meantime, suffering is vital to free us from the grip of egoism, pride and hard-heartedness and to inculcate virtues of humility, gentleness and compassion. Jesus interpreted his sufferings as a self-sacrifice for others, as the greatest act of love (Jn 15:13), and Paul encourages Christians to do the same (Col 1:24). Since eternal life is one of unconditional love, entrance to it requires freedom from egoism, arrogance and domination of others and so suffering can be most helpful in gaining that freedom. It also helps towards becoming more loving, which defines who we are and this identity we take with us to eternal life. God's Spirit will help us to endure suffering and profit from it if we ask for it with perseverance.

The imperfect world in which we live is a vast field in which to make choices that affect ourselves and others in the face of imperfection. We will have to make choices in favour of love, compassion, justice and self-sacrifice that help move us away from egocentricity. We must gradually learn through our choices who we are and how we affect other people. God has given us the freedom to choose and also an imperfect world as an arena in which to make fundamental choices that will form our identity for all eternity. Suffering can become a short-cut to greater love if we choose it to be so. Although suffering is painful and difficult to bear, it can also inspire great love provided we see it through the eyes of faith, with the power of the Spirit and the support and prayers of the Church community. Jesus assures us that his yoke is easy and his burden is light (Mt 11:28–30).[6]

Eucharist

Jesus at the Last Supper interpreted his suffering and death as an offering for sinners to make reparation for sin and as an act of unconditional love (Jn 15:13) in the context of the Jewish Passover feast. He identified the bread as his body and the red wine as his blood poured out for many. The offering of his whole self (*soma*) given for others included the gift of his blood. Since blood was used by the high priest as a sin offering on the great Day of Atonement (Lev 16), Jesus, as the Suffering Servant, made his self-offering into a sin offering (*asham*, Is 53:10) which brings about universal salvation. He also associated himself with the sacrifice of the paschal lamb (Ex 12) which protected the Israelites from death and enabled them to move from slavery to freedom in the Promised Land.

Jesus at the Last Supper directed his disciples to 'do this in memory of me' (1 Cor 11:24) and so it became the ritual whereby the risen Christ's presence with his people is concretised and perpetuated. Christ's body and blood are identified with the bread and wine. Through this presence, the risen Christ brings about the unity of believers who partake of the Eucharist. The liturgy called the Mass by which the risen Christ is made present to nourish believers becomes 'the new covenant in my blood' (1 Cor 11:25), an allusion to the sealing of the covenant at Sinai (Ex 24:8) and the new covenant of Jeremiah (Jer 31:31ff). This proclamation of the Lord's death must continue 'until he comes' (1 Cor 11:26). In this way, Christ in his risen, glorious state fully accomplishes the salvation of those who partake of the table of the Lord throughout the ages until the end of time: 'Anyone who does eat my flesh and drink my blood has eternal life, and I will raise him up on the last day' (Jn 6:54).

Resurrection

The resurrection of Jesus Christ is the central belief of Christianity (1 Cor 15:13–19) as both the foundation of Jesus' claim to be Son of God and as a sign of God's unconditional love for us. The disciples experienced a divinely transformed Jesus who makes his embodiment known through his wounds (Jn 20:28) and 'they knew it was the *Lord*' (Jn 21:12, emphasis added), suggesting Jesus' divine appearance. The appearance of the risen Lord was the chief motivation behind the proclamation of the gospel and the missionary outreach of the early Church. These witnesses had everything to lose and nothing to gain. Why were they prepared to suffer persecution and possible death if their message had been false? The disciples acknowledged that Jesus was risen from the dead, that he was the fulfilment of Israel's prophecies and continued to be their leader through the Spirit. They worshipped Jesus as Lord and associated him with divine status, co-equal with the Father. We may wonder how the early Christian community became the most dynamic missionary movement in the history of religions with an executed Messiah as their sole leader if belief in the resurrection was not central to that proclamation.

Transcendent Destiny[7]

As we have seen, reason alone is insufficient to fully understand our transcendent nature and destiny, for many questions remain unanswered. God himself would have to answer them through his self-revelation. The evidence that Jesus was 'who he said he was' is historically convincing, but not enough by itself to move us to faith. We must feel the need to turn to Jesus as our Saviour to answer life's ultimate questions that arise out of our perceived darkness, self-alienation and incompleteness. If we feel no need or affinity, then the evidence may be interesting but irrelevant to our personal lives. If, on the other hand, we believe that Jesus is God-with-us and decide to follow him, then we are on the path to God's salvation and can hope for an eternity with the all-loving God.

Why is there need for mission and evangelisation? For one thing, all people deserve to know the heart and face of the true God and that the accident of birth does not disqualify them because of God's

Conclusion

universal intention to save. Everybody deserves to know that there is no ultimate tragedy in life and that suffering will be redeemed, that our destiny is to be with an all-loving God and one another for all eternity in perfect love and happiness. If Jesus is the source of the ultimate purpose, destiny, hope and joy, then his followers will want to share it with others, because it can change people and our world for the better. Furthermore, there will be transformation and glorification when we pass from this world to the heavenly realm. Our embodied nature will be brought to perfection, symbolised by the messianic banquet (Is 25:6–9; Lk 13:28–29). Happiness comes from the perfect satisfaction of all our desires by the perfect being we call God.

There is also the possibility of hell as self-exclusion from communion with God and others. God allows us to choose a life of self-absorption and self-idolatry if we wish. For anti-love cannot exist in heaven and God allows our true preferences and desires to determine a state of definitive self-punishment. This is the self-inflicted result of deliberately rejecting love to procure something more intensely desired in the present like fame, power, pleasure, etc. Although God desires to save everyone, he gives each person the freedom to reject him. For God cannot make truly loving creatures unless he allows them the choice to not love, otherwise we would be programmed and not free. Purgatory in the Catholic tradition is regarded as a place of purification after death until the last vestiges of egoism are removed before entering the bliss of eternity.

The return of the Lord at the end of time, which is part of the Christian proclamation, can only be described in images. These images, however, should not be interpreted as objective statements; they are not meant to be a description of the future, but point to the truth of a mysterious consummation. There is no intra-historical fulfilment or perfectibility of the world which modern ideologies proclaim. For immortality does not inhere in human beings or in the material cosmos, but in a relationship with the living God. Hence, human beings are able to live forever because they are capable of having a relationship with One who is eternal. The soul is the capacity for this relationship and in the soul matter attains its completeness in the resurrection of the body.

Concluding Remarks

The meaning of history at its deepest level is, therefore, the history of divine presence and its gradual manifestation in human consciousness in the great foundational experiences and symbolisations of divine presence. The historical symbols endeavour to express the omnipresence with human beings of a God who is substantially hidden. The frontier of that presence gradually becomes luminous for human beings through revelation, culminating in the disclosure of God in Jesus Christ, the image (*eikon*) of the invisible God (Col 1:15) with whom human dignity, meaning and destiny are inextricably linked.

For the believer, Christianity occupies a privileged place in the order of salvation because it was instituted by Christ, the unique manifestation of God who has come to meet us personally at our level. Outside of Christianity, God's human face is unknown; in Christianity, God meets human beings in the human countenance of the man Jesus: 'The Father and I are one' (Jn 10:30). Therefore, the Christian experience of God has a unique character and the transition from non-Christian religions to Christianity brings with it a true, unique newness.

The eagerness for life expressed in hedonism that we find prevalent in contemporary Western society has paradoxically given rise to a culture of death which is becoming more and more its defining characteristic. The elimination of God from public life has generated a fear that lurks beneath the surface of modern existence. People have hopes for the future expressed in a secular faith in progress through technology that is regarded as freedom from the constraints of the world and history alike. This goal, however, is illusory and unattainable, for human beings are not God. There will be no healing of our culture if God is not again recognised as the foundation of our entire existence. Only in union with God is human life truly life.

> We are not simply hollow men and women, empty husks of humanity wandering without guidance, capable only of inflicting unlimited misery on one another. Within us is a movement of resistance, rooted in the reality of our transcendent dimension, and capable of filling our lives with its truth and direction if we

responsibly follow its promptings. Humanity is not alone. We are part of the community of the spirit that mysteriously reaches its apex in the divine Being itself.[8]

With the waning of rationalism in Western culture and the advent of post-modernism (1989–), there is a new emphasis on the importance of story and image that appeals to the imagination. Post-modernity is more interested in narrative than in rational argument and this offers an opening for a biblically based anthropology. Biblical stories and images have powerful imaginative, moral and aesthetic appeal. The reduction of historical accounts and narratives to timeless ideas has to a great extent lost its appeal today. The Christian story of creation, fall, redemption and consummation has the capacity to change lives, gives reasons for living and hope for the future. It answers questions of who we are, where we are going, how to get there, what is wrong with our world and what is the solution. Images rather than concepts are a better means of communication because of what they connote, suggest and point towards: 'Reason is the organ of truth, imagination is the organ of meaning' (C.S. Lewis).

Since access to reality today is primarily visual rather than rational, there are the rich, emotional, imaginative, moral and existential aspects to Christianity as well as the rational that need to be retrieved. Imagination, for example, helps us to visualise how things fit together through patterns of relationships that help explain what we observe. Christianity affirms that there is a broader vision of reality beyond the limits of reason, yet capable of being recognised as reasonable once it is grasped. The notion of divine revelation concerns a view of reality that lies beyond the capacity of human reason to fully grasp. It is an illumination of our world so that we can see things more clearly. Christianity offers a richer, more satisfying account of our world that encompasses the relational, aesthetic, emotional and imaginative aspects of living. Since love, trust and commitment belong within personal relationships, we come to realise that we have to trust rather than prove our core beliefs as committed Christians.

That human living requires spiritual foundations is clear from our contemporary wasteland mired in violence, corruption, terrorism and hopelessness. The existence of God and the importance of classical philosophy and Judeo-Christian revelation need to be reaffirmed in the light of the spiritual chaos brought about by secularism in the twentieth century. Classical and biblical resources must be re-employed to renew public life, otherwise the foundations of freedom will continue to crumble before our eyes.

> The answer to the question of human origins, then, is that each human being is constituted into existence as a you-for-You in one cooperative act: creation by an unlimited and personal source and co-creation by the child's parents. Each human being outweighs the Big Bang; each human being is a new beginning of a new personal universe. Nothing less would be a sufficient answer.[9]

As embodied, human beings are rooted in over 13 billion years of material history of the universe and 4 billion years of biological evolutionary history on this earth. With the advent of human consciousness, though, there is discontinuity with the non-human world, for human existence is also independent of its biological basis. Hence the importance of a sense of the unique and irreplaceable worth of every human being. Indeed, the whole of humanity may be considered as one family capable of being united as 'we' because of its groundedness in a trans-finite 'You':

> What unites all human beings is the capacity to reach out to and be drawn by the transcendent, not that we are genetically united since 150,000 years ago. If mankind is to have a history, its members must be able to respond to the movement of divine presence in their souls.[10]

This alone becomes the basis for the creation of a universal dialogue when we reach out together in a genuine search for truth, justice and love to those who are different from us. 'Things do not happen in the astrophysical universe; the universe together with all things founded in it, happens in God.'[11] God it is who is the origin and destiny of each human being and of the whole universe.

So my heart exults, my soul rejoices,
my body, too, will rest securely,
for you will not abandon my soul to Sheol,
nor allow the one you love to see the Pit,
you will reveal the path of life to me,
give me unbounded joy in your presence,
and at your right hand everlasting pleasures.

Psalm 16:9–11

'Behold, the dwelling of God is with men. He will dwell with them, and they shall be his people, and God himself will be with them; he will wipe away every tear from their eyes, and death shall be no more, for the former things have passed away.' And he who sat on the throne said, 'Behold, I make all things new.'

Revelation 21:3–5

Endnotes

1   For this section I am following Robert Spitzer, *The Soul's Upward Yearning: Clues to our Transcendent Nature from Experience and Reason*, San Francisco: Ignatius Press, 2015.

2   St Augustine, *Confessions*, 1.

3   For further reading, see Gavin D'Costa (ed.), *The Catholic Church and the World Religions: A Theological and Phenomenological Account*, London: T&T Clark, 2011.

4   Joseph Ratzinger, *Faith and the Future*, San Francisco: Ignatius Press, 2019, p. 33.

5   Joseph Ratzinger, *Introduction to Christianity*, San Francisco: Ignatius Press, 2004, p. 80.

6   Robert Spitzer, Robin A Bernhoft and Camille E. de Blasi, *Healing the Culture: A Commonsense Philosophy of Happiness, Freedom and the Life Issues*, San Francisco: Ignatius Press, 2000, pp. 159–192.

7   I am indebted here to Robert Spitzer, *God So Loved the World: Clues to our Transcendent Destiny from the Revelation of Jesus*, San Francisco: Ignatius Press, 2016, pp. 146–186.

8   David Walsh, *After Ideology: Recovering the Spiritual Foundations of Freedom*, New York: Harper Collins, 1990, p. 277.

9   *Ibid.*, p. 319.

10   Eric Voegelin, *Order and History, vol. 4: The Ecumenic Age*, Baton Rouge: LSUP, 1974, p. 305.

11   *Ibid.*, p. 333–334.

SELECT BIBLIOGRAPHY

Abbott, W.M., *The Documents of Vatican II*, London: Geoffrey Chapman, 1966.

Anderson, B.W., *Contours of Old Testament Theology*, Minneapolis: Fortress Press, 1999.

Anderson, B.W., Bishop, S., and Newman, J., *Understanding the Old Testament*, 5th edn, New Jersey: Prentice Hall, 2007.

Barrett, C.K., *The First Epistle to the Corinthians*, 2nd edn, London: A&C Black, 1971.

Bergsma, J., and Pitre, B., *A Catholic Introduction to the Bible: Old Testament*, San Francisco: Ignatius Press, 2018.

Birch, B.C., Brueggemann, W., Fretheim, T.E., and Petersen, D.L., *A Theological Introduction to the Old Testament*, Nashville: Abingdon Press, 2005.

Blenkinsopp, J., *A History of Prophecy in Israel*, revised and enlarged edn, Louisville, KY: Westminster John Knox Press, 1996.

Brown, R.E., *The Gospel According to John*, 2 vols., Anchor Bible (29, 29A), New York: Doubleday, 1966, 1970.

———— *An Introduction to the New Testament,* New York: Doubleday, 1997.

Brown, R.E., Fitzmyer, J.A., and Murphy, R.E., eds., *The New Jerome Biblical Commentary*, New Jersey: Prentice Hall, 1990.

Childs, B.S., *Introduction to the Old Testament as Scripture*, London: SCM Press, 1979.

Crenshaw, J.L., *Old Testament Wisdom: An Introduction*, Atlanta: Westminster John Knox Press, 1999.

D'Costa, G., ed., *The Catholic Church and the World Religions: A Theological and Phenomenological Account*, London: T&T Clark, 2011.

Deidun, T.J., *New Covenant Morality in Paul*, Rome: Biblical Institute Press, 1981.

Duggan, M.W., *The Consuming Fire: A Christian Guide to the Old Testament*, updated and revised edn, Huntington: Our Sunday Visitor, 2005.

Dunn, J.D.G., *The Theology of Paul the Apostle*, Edinburgh: T&T Clark, 1998.

Fitzmyer, J.A., *Romans*, Anchor Bible (33), London: Geoffrey Chapman, 1993.

Gnilka, J., *Jesus of Nazareth: Message and History*, Peabody, MA; Hendrickson Publishers, 1997.

Gorman, M.J., *Apostle of the Crucified Lord: A Theological Introduction to Paul and his Letters*, Grand Rapids: W.B. Eerdmans, 2004.

Habel, N.C., *The Book of Job: A Commentary*, London: SCM Press, 1985.

Harrington, D.J., *Jesus Ben Sira of Jerusalem*, Collegeville, Minnesota: Liturgical Press, 2005.

Hogan, M., *The Biblical Vision of the Human Person: Implications for a Philosophical Anthropology*, Frankfurt am Mein: Peter Lang, 1994.

————— *The Four Gospels: Following in the Footsteps of Jesus*, Dublin: Veritas, 2015.

John Paul II, *Man and Woman He Created Them: A Theology of the Body*, Boston: Pauline Books & Media, 2006.

Kiely, B.M., *Psychology and Moral Theology*, Rome: Gregorian University Press, 1980.

Kraus, H.-J., *Theology of the Psalms*, Minneapolis: Augsburg, 1986.

—— *Psalms 1–59*, Minneapolis: Augsburg, 1988.

—— *Psalms 60–150*, Minneapolis: Augsburg, 1989.

Leahy, B., and Walsh, D., eds., *The Human Voyage of Self-Discovery*, Dublin: Veritas, 2013.

Leclerc, T.L., *Introduction to the Prophets: Their Stories, Sayings and Scrolls,* New York: Paulist Press, 2007.

Lohfink, G., *Jesus of Nazareth: What He Wanted, Who He Was*, trans. L.M. Maloney, Collegeville, Minnesota: The Liturgical Press, 2012.

—— *Is This All There Is?*, trans. L.M. Maloney, Collegeville, Minnesota: The Liturgical Press, 2017.

Lohfink, N., *Qoheleth: A Continental Commentary*, Minneapolis: Fortress, 2003.

Lonergan, B.J.F., *Insight: A Study of Human Understanding*, London: Longmans, 1961.

—— *Method in Theology*, London: DLT, 1972.

Matthews, V.H., *101 Questions and Answers on the Historical Books of the Bible*, New Jersey: Paulist Press, 2009.

McKeating, C., *Light which Dims the Stars: A Christian Theology of Creation*, Makati: St Paul's Philippines, 2015.

Miller, J.W., *Meet the Prophets*, New York: Paulist Press, 1987.

Moule, C.F.D., 'St Paul and Dualism: The Pauline Conception of Resurrection', *New Testament Studies*, 12/2, 1966.

Mullins, M., *The Gospel of John: A Commentary*, Dublin: Columba Press, 2003.

—— *The Gospel of Mark: A Commentary*, Dublin: Columba Press, 2005.

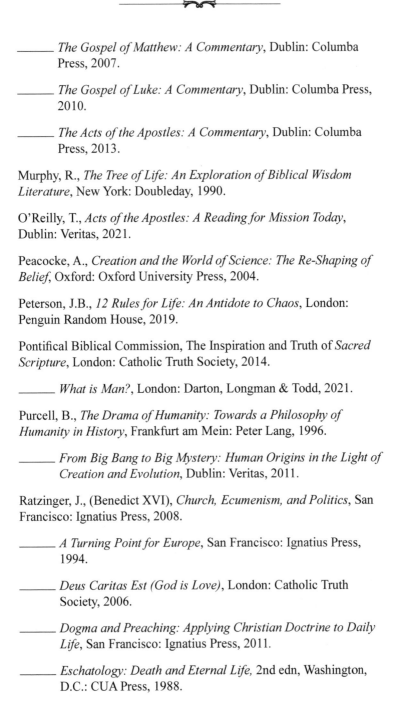

_____ *The Gospel of Matthew: A Commentary*, Dublin: Columba Press, 2007.

_____ *The Gospel of Luke: A Commentary*, Dublin: Columba Press, 2010.

_____ *The Acts of the Apostles: A Commentary*, Dublin: Columba Press, 2013.

Murphy, R., *The Tree of Life: An Exploration of Biblical Wisdom Literature*, New York: Doubleday, 1990.

O'Reilly, T., *Acts of the Apostles: A Reading for Mission Today*, Dublin: Veritas, 2021.

Peacocke, A., *Creation and the World of Science: The Re-Shaping of Belief*, Oxford: Oxford University Press, 2004.

Peterson, J.B., *12 Rules for Life: An Antidote to Chaos*, London: Penguin Random House, 2019.

Pontifical Biblical Commission, The Inspiration and Truth of *Sacred Scripture*, London: Catholic Truth Society, 2014.

_____ *What is Man?*, London: Darton, Longman & Todd, 2021.

Purcell, B., *The Drama of Humanity: Towards a Philosophy of Humanity in History*, Frankfurt am Mein: Peter Lang, 1996.

_____ *From Big Bang to Big Mystery: Human Origins in the Light of Creation and Evolution*, Dublin: Veritas, 2011.

Ratzinger, J., (Benedict XVI), *Church, Ecumenism, and Politics*, San Francisco: Ignatius Press, 2008.

_____ *A Turning Point for Europe*, San Francisco: Ignatius Press, 1994.

_____ *Deus Caritas Est (God is Love)*, London: Catholic Truth Society, 2006.

_____ *Dogma and Preaching: Applying Christian Doctrine to Daily Life*, San Francisco: Ignatius Press, 2011.

_____ *Eschatology: Death and Eternal Life,* 2nd edn, Washington, D.C.: CUA Press, 1988.

_____ *Faith and the Future*, San Francisco: Ignatius Press, 2019.

_____ *Fundamental Speeches from Five Decades*, San Francisco: Ignatius Press, 2012.

_____ *Introduction to Christianity*, San Francisco: Ignatius Press, 2004.

_____ *Jesus of Nazareth: From the Baptism in the Jordan to the Transfiguration*, New York: Doubleday, 2007.

_____ *Jesus of Nazareth: Holy Week*, San Francisco: Ignatius Press, 2011.

_____ *Jesus of Nazareth: The Infancy Narratives*, New York: Bloomsbury, 2012.

_____ *Principles of Catholic Theology: Building Stones for a Fundamental Theology*, San Francisco: Ignatius Press, 2012.

_____ *Truth and Tolerance: Christian Belief and World Religions*, San Francisco: Ignatius Press, 2004.

Rowley, H.H., *Worship in Ancient Israel: Its Forms and Meaning*, London: SPCK, 1978.

Sarna, N.M., *Understanding Genesis*, New York: Schocken Books, 1970.

Schall, J.V., *At the Limits of Political Philosophy*, Washington, D.C.: CUA Press, 1996.

Schnackenburg, R., *Jesus in the Gospels: A Biblical Christology*, Louisville, KY: Westminster John Knox Press, 1995.

Seow, C.-L., *Ecclesiastes*, Anchor Bible, New York: Doubleday, 1997.

Spitzer, R., *The Soul's Upward Yearning: Clues to Our Transcendent Nature from Experience and Reason*, San Francisco: Ignatius Press, 2015.

_____ *God So Loved the World: Clues to Our Transcendent Destiny from the Revelation of Jesus*, San Francisco: Ignatius Press, 2016.

Spitzer, R., Bernhoft, R.A., and de Blasi, C.E., *Healing the Culture: A Commonsense Philosophy of Happiness, Freedom and the Life Issues*, San Francisco: Ignatius Press, 2000.

Stamm, J.J., and Andrew, M.E., *The Ten Commandments in Recent Research,* London: SCM Press, 1967.

Stanley, D., 'Christ, the Last Adam,' in Michael J. Taylor (ed.), *A Companion to Paul: Readings in Pauline Theology*, New York: Alba House, 1975.

Vawter, B., *On Genesis: A New Reading,* London: Geoffrey Chapman, 1977.

Von Rad, G., *Genesis: A Commentary*, London: SCM Press, 1963.

_____ *Wisdom in Israel*, London: SCM Press, 1972.

_____ *The Message of the Prophets*, London: SCM Press, 1968.

Voegelin, E., *Order and History, vol. 4: The Ecumenic Age*, Baton Rouge: Louisiana University Press, 1974.

_____ *Published Essays 1966–1985 (The Collected Works of Eric Voegelin, vol. 12),* (E. Sandoz, ed.), Baton Rouge: Louisiana University Press, 1990.

_____ *What is History? and Other Late Unpublished Writings (The Collected Works of Eric Voegelin, vol. 28)*, (T.A. Hollweck, P. Caringella, eds.), Baton Rouge: Louisiana University Press, 1990.

_____ *Order and History, vol. 1: Israel and Revelation (The Collected Works of Eric Voegelin, vol. 14),* (M. Hogan, ed.), Columbia: University of Missouri Press, 2001.

Walsh, D., *After Ideology: Recovering the Spiritual Foundations of Freedom*, San Francisco: HarperCollins, 1996.

_____ *Guarded by Mystery: Meaning in a Postmodern Age*, Washington, D.C.: CUA Press, 1999.

Westermann, C., *Genesis 1–11: A Commentary*, London: SPCK, 1984.

_____ *Genesis 12–36: A Commentary*, London: SPCK, 1986.

Winston, D., *The Wisdom of Solomon*, The Anchor Bible, New York: Doubleday, 1999.